AF441743

OUR FEARS MATTER TO GOD

BY JOHN W BOLAND

BOOK / BIBLE STUDY

Published in the United states of America
ISBN: 9798639937132
Imprint: Independently published

1.Religion / Christian Life / Professional growth
2.Religion / Christian Ministry / Evangelism

TABLE OF CONTENTS

INTRODUCTION

How do you explain fear, how do you describe the sensation of overwhelming fear? Who can put into words the reality of uncontrollable terror so that everyone can understand?

According to Psychology Today, fear is a vital response to physical and emotional danger.[i] That danger can either be real or imagined. Phobias, on the other hand, fall into five broad categories:

1.   Animals, such as a fear of spiders, dogs, or bugs.
2.   Natural environment, such as a fear of heights or storms.
3.   Blood, injury, and injection, such as a fear of needles or medical procedures.
4.   Situational, such as a fear of storms, flying or riding in elevators.
5.   Other, such as a fear of vomiting or choking

God's Word says that there is no room in a believers' life for fear of anything, because love overcomes everything![ii] Christ-like love based on God's Word banishes any idea of worry, anxiety, distress, panic, fear of public speaking, elevators, spiders, or the very idea of dread. The reality is that the very idea of being afraid of anything is a tool of the devil. It is calculated to cripple normal life. It is intended to control the individual through their reasonable thoughts, words, or deeds. Are you anxious about going outside, concerned over making a mistake, upset because something is out of order, terrified of storms, or distressed thinking about death?   All these inner thoughts are not based on rational thinking or God's love.

Fear is powerful and primitive. Fear tells us when we are in danger. Fear has been divided into two types of responses.

1. *Biochemical*
   a. The universally known "fight or flight" response.
2. *Emotional*
   a. This is based on individuality.[iii] It ranges from the thrill of the Xtreme Sports to the debilitating fear of circumstances, conditions, or environments.

Is fear justifiable? According to the Medical News Today it can be.[iv] When we hear unexplainable noises. When we are in dangerous or hostile situations. When strong storms are battering our home during a weather alert day.   However, there are times when it can be inappropriate. When watching a scary movie. When our lives are taken over by illogical and intense anxiety disorders. Phobias do not come with rational rules of order or placement. At times they are easy to anticipate and recognize. The question, for those who suffer from these unpleasant and life interfering experiences, is how to deal with it and control it rather than allowing it to control the individual and sometimes those around them.

CHAPTER 1:
FEAR DEFINED
&
EXPLAINED

According to Merriam-Webster dictionary fear[v] is simply an unpleasant strong emotion brought about when someone anticipates or becomes aware of danger and acts or responds in involuntarily even if there is no obvious immediate danger.

The Mayo Clinic[vi] defines fear in much the same way. As an unpleasant feeling triggered by the perceived danger, real or imagined. They suggest several possibilities of treatment from basic self-help, from breathing into a bag or talking with friends.   If conditions warrant it, they suggest considering getting regular clinical help.

The Mayo Clinic goes further into the subject by addressing the serious issue of anxiety disorder. This is a more serious mental health disorder which is characterized by strong feelings of worry, anxiety, or apprehension. This level of emotional stress interferes with daily living. Examples of this condition include:

- Panic Attacks,
- Obsessive-Compulsive Disorder,
- Post-Traumatic Stress Disorder.

Symptoms include emotions out of proportion to the events' impact, inability to calm a worry, and uncontrollable restlessness. Treatment at this level would require counseling and possibly medication. It was said that this condition is considered very common with more than 3 million US cases per year.[vii]

Post-Traumatic Stress Disorder is a condition which makes it difficult for a person to recover from most terrifying events. This can last from months or years. "Triggers" can bring back memories of the trauma and their intense emotional and physical reactions. Symptoms range anywhere from:

- Nightmares,
- Unwanted memories,
- Avoidance of situations or near conditions,
- Heightened reactions,
- Anxiety,
- Moodiness.

Current treatment options are psychotherapy, medications to symptom management.

According to the University of Minnesota Health & Well-being page[viii] the impact of chronic fear is unhealthy. Living with any of these conditions has serious health consequences. Medical studies have shown that response to fear weakens the immune system causes heart damage and stomach problems. It can speed up ageing and even shorten a persons' life.

Furthermore, fear can affect long-term memory. It has been known to cause brain damage. If you know anyone suffering from this condition, then you know it leaves them anxious most of the time. To someone in a more intense level of fear, the world looks scary, and their memories confirm it.

Eventually. uncontrolled fear interferes with emotions, the ability to read non-verbal cues and other information necessary for effective communication between friends and family. It impacts how we think, our decision-making ability, leaves us vulnerable to irrational emotions and impulsiveness. All this can leave us unable to act right.

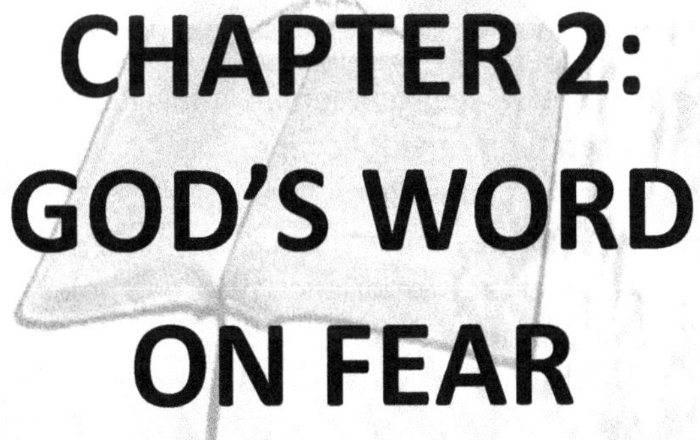

CHAPTER 2:
GOD'S WORD ON FEAR

So, what can we, mere humans say about our fears that God hasn't already addressed in His Word? First of all, if you do not believe in God you are in a sad state of affairs.

- Your fears can overwhelm you.
- Your fears could even control your life.
- Your fears can damage relationships.

There is hope, you have choices before you to fix that unexplainable and uncontrollable pain of fear!

1. If you are relying on Human Intelligence then you will need to ask the following:
   a. Human counseling
      i. Do they understand & connect?
      ii. Did they experience the deep hole?
   b. Medication
      i. Is it addictive?
      ii. Are there side effects?

2. If your idea of God is controlling, bigotted, misogynist, and restricted then you must not have read His Word.

God's existence is centered around the idea of sacrificial love. He loves us (you and me) so much that He has been attempting to create a relationship with us. Yes, a connection where the two of us understand each other. An unbreakable bond not a religion. Not an organization where some potentate, chieftain, organizer, founder, superior, religious bully, or person-in-charge makes up the rules to control our everyday lives and gives weekly lectures on how to comply with those rules. He even sent a part of Himself to earth in the person of Jesus Christ to restore that relationship and help us understand and realize the deepest desire of His heart.

3. If you are relying on God, His Word, & Discipleship then you avail yourself to such things as:

Wisdom,	Endurance,
Honesty,	Righteousness,
Patience,	Understanding,
Strength,	True Goodness,
True Love,	Encouragement,
Knowledge,	True Relationships,
Confidence,	Inner Peace.

In order to even begin to overcome our fears we must start with respecting the God of creation because that is the beginning of wisdom. Seeking wisdom means we begin to depart from everything that is evil. This means we focus less on our fears, both the explainable and unexplainable because they put us ineffective to do anything good.[ix] We must focus more on understanding who God is, what God is about and why God wants a relationship with us in the first place.

We must also understand a few things about overcoming anxiety:

- We should fear God, more than the problems we face in life.[x]
- We should not mock God.
  - It promises to bring about worse results than we think we can handle.[xi]
- In God is found strength, calm, & comfort, not helplessness, stress, & worry.[xii]
- In God there is peace & order, not chaos, confusion, & disorder.
- Yielding to fear shows a lack of confidence in our relationship with God.
- Living through a disaster means God has a future of living planned.
- Once a new normal is established new ministry opportunities present themselves.

Scripture makes it clear that fearing God is the only appropriate emotion to life's issues. The fear of God saves & protects us, our family and keeps us from caving into a sinful habit or lifestyle. There is a difference between being known as a "church-attender" and "God-fearing" The very idea that anyone is "God-fearing" means they are trustworthy, keeps their word, is kind & compassionate toward others.[xiii]

BIBLE STUDY

Job 28:28

The fear of the Lord, that is wisdom; and to depart from evil is understanding.

Psalm 34:7

The angel of the Lord encamped round about them that fear Him and delivered them.

Psalm 56:4

In God I will praise His word,

in God I have put my trust,

I will not fear what flesh can do unto me.

Psalm 112:1

Blessed is the man that fears the Lord, that delights greatly in His commandments.

Psalm 147:11

The Lord taketh pleasure in them that fear him, in those that hope in His mercy.

Proverbs 1:7

The fear of the Lord is the beginning of knowledge: but fools despise wisdom and instruction.

Proverbs 3:7

Be not wise in thine own eyes:

fear the Lord and depart from evil.

Proverbs 10:27

The fear of the Lord prolongs days: but the years of the wicked shall be shortened.

Proverbs 14:16

A wise man fears, and departs from evil:

but the fool rages, and is confident.

Proverbs 14:26

In the fear of the Lord is strong confidence: and his children shall have a place of refuge.

Proverbs 15:16
> Better is little with the fear of the Lord than great treasure and trouble therewith.

Proverbs 23:17
> Let not thine heart envy sinners: but be thou in the fear of the Lord all day long.

Proverbs 24:21
> My son, fear thou the Lord and the king: and meddle not with them that are given to change:

Proverbs 29:25
> The fear of man bringeth a snare: but whoso puts his trust in the Lord shall be safe.

Proverbs 31:30
> Favor is deceitful, and beauty is vain: but a woman that fears the Lord, she shall be praised.

Please answer the following questions:
- What are we to do with our fears?
- What fear is appropriate?
- What happens when fear is misguided?

BOLAND

FEARS

CHAPTER 3: BIBLICAL CHARACTERS & FEAR

FEARS

Adam & Eve

Adam & Eve became fearful after they conducted themselves in violation of God's Word to Adam. Adam obviously shared with Eve what was expected of them. However, they were lured away from this understanding of the reality of God's Truth. The truth is they listened to something other than God and fell into temptation of that which was forbidden. For them it was fruit, for us today it is any number of material things. For Adam & Eve the reality hit when they realized the following things and not necessarily in this order:

1. They were naked,
2. They had done wrong,
3. They had broken God's command,
4. Their relationship with God was broken,
5. They were afraid of the coming consequences.

They, at first, hid from God. Isn't that what most people in our world do today? Hide their sins in fear and shame, hoping no one finds out or confronts them? Adam eventually confessed what had happened, only when confronted by God. Isn't that how we do it; live with the fear of exposure just hoping no one ever finds out? Adam finally confessed that they hid themselves because they were afraid of God finding out. God, out of His infinite love, sought them out to calm their fears. God, out of His infinite love, did not blame anyone. Adam did! Isn't that the same today? It seems we live in an age of no responsibility. In other words, it is never our fault for the wrongs we do! It is always something from our past, the environment or someone else made us do it. God, in His infinite love, reduced their stress of being naked by clothing them. Nevertheless, God, through His infinite justice, allowed the consequences of their conduct to be carried out. However, it is also obvious from God's Word that in His infinite love, He continued to pursue a love relationship with both them and their family. This is the same God who wants to calm our fears and pursue a love relationship with us today.

The point of the story is as follows:
- God wants a relationship with humanity,
- God seeks the best for humanity,
- Humanity has nothing to fear from God,
- The emotion of fear is not a Godly characteristic,
- Satan will deceive humanity in believing lies about God.

FEARS

BIBLE STUDY

<u>The Love-Relationship</u>

Genesis 3:9-10, 21

The Lord God called unto Adam, and said unto him:
- Where art thou?

He (Adam) said:
- I heard thy voice in the garden,
- I was afraid because I was naked,
- I hid myself.

  Unto Adam also and to his wife did the Lord God make coats of skins and clothed them.

<u>The Justice & Consequences</u>

Genesis 3: 17 -19, 23-24

Unto Adam He (God) said:
- Because thou hast harkened unto the voice of thy wife,
- Hast eaten of the tree, of which I commanded thee, saying,
- Thou shalt not eat of it:
  - Cursed is the ground for thy sake,
  - In sorrow shalt thou eat of it all the days of thy life,
  - Thorns also and thistles shall it bring forth to thee,
  - Thou shalt eat the herb of the field,

- o In the sweat of thy face shalt thou eat bread, till thou return unto the ground,
- o For out of it were thou taken, for dust thou art, and unto dust shalt thou return.

Therefore, the Lord God sent him forth from the garden of Eden, to till the ground from whence he was taken. So, he drove out the man, and he placed at the east of the garden of Eden Cherubim and a flaming sword, which turned every way, to keep the way of the tree of life.

Please answer the following questions:
- Why do we hide ourselves in times of fear?
- Why do we blame others rather than accept fault?
- Why do some in our society think consequences for bad conduct is wrong?

FEARS

Cain & Abel

The story of Cain & Able is the classic brother love-hate relationship. They both brought offerings to God. Able it is said brought the firstlings. Cain brought the fruit of the ground.

- What makes the difference?
- Why was Able's offering respected by God and Cain's not?
- What was Cain supposed to do after being rejected by God?
- Was God's punishment reasonable, just & sufficient or was it cruel & unusual?

How God looked on each of them made an emotional wreck of Cain to the point of jealousy & anger. At the onset of these emotions God warned Cain that sin is just waiting to gain entrance by such an emotional outburst. God called Cain's mood a tantrum, even accused him of sulking. This apparently was not what Cain wanted to hear and he snapped, thus killing Abel. At that point fear entered into Can's life. He felt that the punishment did not meet the crime. He also feared that people would be on the look out to hunt him down and kill him.

The point of the story is as follows:
- God wants our first and best not our just OK.
- Negative emotions only lead to bad decisions.
- The idea of criticism is not disapproval.

BIBLE STUDY

<u>Cain & Abel</u>

Genesis 4:3-5

In process of time it came to pass, Cain brought:
- The fruit of the ground an offering unto the Lord.
  - Unto Cain and to his offering God had not respect
  - And Cain was very wroth, and his countenance fell.

Abel, brought:
- The firstlings of his flock and the fat thereof.
  - The Lord had respect unto Abel and to his offering.

Genesis 4: 6-7

The Lord said unto Cain:
- Why art thou wroth?
- Why is thy countenance fallen?
- If thou do well, shalt thou not be accepted.
- If thou do not well, sin lieth at the door.
- Unto thee shall be his desire, and thou shalt rule over him.

Genesis 6: 8-11

Cain talked with Abel his brother. It came to pass, when they were in the field that Cain rose up against Abel his brother and slew him.

Lord said unto Cain:
- Where is Abel thy brother?

He (Cain) said:
- I know not.
- Am I my brother's keeper?

He (God) said:
- What hast thou done?
- The voice of thy brother's blood cries unto Me from the ground.
- Now art thou cursed from the earth which hath opened her mouth to receive thy brother's blood from thy hand.

Genesis 6:13-14

Cain said unto the Lord:
- My punishment is greater than I can bear.
- Behold, thou hast driven me out this day from the face of the earth.
- From thy face shall I be hid.
- I shall be a fugitive and a vagabond in the earth.

Please answer the following questions:
- Why wasn't Cain's offering good enough?
- What do you think was the difference?
- Did the punishment fit the crime?

BOLAND

FEARS

45

Abraham & God

Consider the case pf Abram /Abraham.
Approximately 2,000 + years after the fall of Babel and the confusion of language Abram was born. Then in his 75th year, appeared and directed him to move to the "promised land" of Cannon. This was at a time when moving in that manner was unusual. He listened to God. He traveled throughout the Middle East. The Scriptures never mention fear concerning these moves, except in Egypt. His travel to Egypt came at a time that a famine took place and was ravaging the land. What made this place unique was his wife! Abram feared what they might do to him, because of pharaoh's desire for her beauty. This caused him and Sarai to lie about their real relationship. Up to that time, there was no mention of him ever being afraid or misleading others. Isn't that just like us? We seem to fear more of what others could do to us than God's Word, God's Promises, or the consequences of breaking God's order. Fear of others provides opportunity for us to do things out of character. The rest of the story is that God took care of Abraham in Egypt and everywhere he travelled

The point of the story is as follows:
- A real encounter with God removes all doubt & fear.
- A relationship with God through Jesus Christ brings peace & contentment.
- A relationship with God overcomes the fear of man.

BIBLE STUDY

<u>God's Promise of Safety & Blessing</u>

Genesis 12:1-4

Now the Lord had said unto Abram,
Get thee out of thy country, and from thy kindred, and from thy father's house, unto a land that I will show thee:
- I will make of thee a great nation.
- I will bless thee and make thy name great,
  - Thou shalt be a blessing.
- I will bless them that bless thee,
  - I will curse him that curses thee.
- In thee shall all families of the earth be blessed.

<u>God's Promise of Land</u>

Genesis 12:6-7

And Abram passed through the land unto the place of Sichem, unto the plain of Moreh. And the Canaanite was then in the land. And the Lord appeared unto Abram, and said,
- Thy seed will I give this land.
- There built he an altar unto the Lord,
  - Who appeared unto him!

The Irrational Fear of Man

Genesis 12:10-13

And there was a famine in the land and Abram went down into Egypt to sojourn there; for the famine was grievous in the land. It came to pass, when he was come near to enter into Egypt, that:
- He (Abram) said unto Sarai his wife,
    - Behold now, I know that thou art a fair woman to look upon.
    - Therefore, it shall come to pass, when the Egyptians shall see thee, that they shall say, this is his wife and they will kill me, but they will save thee alive.
- Say, I pray thee, thou art my sister that it may be well with me for thy sake and my soul shall live because of thee.

God's Promise of Land Renewed

Genesis 13:14-18

And the Lord said unto Abram, after that Lot was separated from him,
- Lift up now thine eyes, and look from the place where thou art northward, and southward, and eastward, and westward
- For all the land which thou see, to thee will I give it, and to thy seed forever.
- I will make thy seed as the dust of the earth: so that if a man can number the dust of the earth, then shall thy seed also be numbered.

<u>A Man of Principle</u>

Genesis 14:18-24

And Melchizedek king of Salem brought forth bread and wine, he was the priest of the most high God:
- He (Melchizedek) blessed him (Abram).
  - Blessed be Abram of the most high God, possessor of heaven and earth
  - Blessed be the most high God, which hath delivered thine enemies into thy hand.
- And he (Abram) gave him tithes of all.
- The king of Sodom said unto Abram,
  - Give me the persons, and (you) take the goods to thyself.
- Abram said to the king of Sodom,
  - I have lift up mine hand unto the Lord, the most high God, the possessor of heaven and earth, that,
  - I will not take from a thread even to a shoe latchet,
  - I will not take any thing that is thine, lest thou shouldest say, I have made Abram rich.
  - Save only that which the young men have eaten, and the portion of the men...

God's Promise of a Son

Genesis 15:1-17

After these things, the word of the Lord came unto Abram in a vision, saying, Fear not, Abram:

- I am thy shield, and thy exceeding great reward.

Abram said:

- Lord God, what wilt thou give me, seeing I go childless, and the steward of my house is this Eliezer of Damascus?

Abram said:

- Behold, to me thou hast given no seed and
- Lo, one born in my house is mine heir.

Behold, the word of the Lord came unto him saying:

- This shall not be thine heir!
- He that shall come forth out of thine own bowels shall be thine heir.
- He believed in the Lord and
    - He counted it to him for righteousness.

God's Covenant

Genesis 17:1-3, 5

And when Abram was ninety years old and nine, God appeared to Abram, and said:
- I am the Almighty God,
- Walk before me and be thou perfect.
- I will make my covenant between me & thee,
- I will multiply thee exceedingly.
- Abram fell on his face.

God talked with him:
- Neither shall thy name any more be called Abram.
- Thy name shall be Abraham,
  - For a father of many nations have I made thee.

Please answer the following questions:
- Why would we fear any human?
- What does it mean to fear what others could do to us?
- What should we do when that type of fear overtakes us?

BOLAND

FEARS

55

Jacob & God

Then there is the case of Jacob. Trouble from the beginning. A momma's boy. Later God would change his name to Israel. The patriarch of the Israelites. He started life by grabbing his brothers heal at birth. He had Esau swear his birthright away over a simple meal. He later sealed the deal by deceiving his blind dying father into believing he was Esau. Then he fled in fear of retaliation. He even fled from his father-in-law due to the older gentleman's double cross, causing him to marry the older homelier daughter first and dragging out his ability to marry the one he originally wanted to marry. He would later fear for his life, when returning home to face his brother years after dealing him dirty on his father's death bed. In studying Jacob, we find that his fears were actually unwarranted because God blessed him, God protected him, and God met his needs in all of life's matters.

The point of the story is as follows:
- A troubled life only brings fear.
- A relationship with God settles all fears.
- A life relying on God's Word brings blessings, protection & contentment.

BIBLE STUDY

<u>Jacob & Esau</u>

Genesis 25:29-34

And Jacob sod pottage and Esau came from the field, and he was faint.

Esau said to Jacob:
- Feed me, I pray thee, with that same red pottage, for I am faint.
    - o   Therefore, was his name called Edom.

Jacob said,
- Sell me this day thy birthright.

Esau said,
- Behold, I am at the point to die and
- What profit shall this birthright do to me?

Jacob said,
- Swear to me this day and he swore unto him,
- He sold his birthright unto Jacob.
- Then Jacob gave Esau bread and pottage of lentils.
- He (Esau) did eat and drink, and rose up, and went his way, thus,
    - o   Esau despised his birthright.

Jacob & His Mother's Deception

Genesis 27:18-30

And he (Jacob) came unto his father, and said:
- My father

He (Isaac) said, here am I:
- who art thou, my son?

Jacob said unto his father:
- I am Esau thy first born.

Isaac said unto Jacob,
- Come near, I pray thee, that I may feel thee, my son, whether thou be my very son Esau or not.
- Jacob went near unto Isaac his father.

He (Issacs) felt him, and said:0
- The voice is Jacob's voice,
    - But the hands are the hands of Esau
    - Art thou my very son Esau?

He (Jacob) said:
- I am.

He (Jacob) came near, and Issacs kissed him and smelled the smell of his raiment, and blessed him, and said:

- Therefore, God give thee of the dew of heaven, and the fatness of the earth, and plenty of corn and wine.
- Let people serve thee, and nations bow down to thee,
- Be lord over thy brethren and let thy mother's sons bow down to thee,
- Cursed be everyone that curses thee,
- Blessed be he that blesses thee.

And it came to pass, as soon as Isaac had made an end of blessing Jacob, that Esau his brother came in from his hunting.

Jacob meeting with his brother

Genesis 27:41

Esau hated Jacob because of the blessing wherewith his father blessed him. Esau said in his heart:
- The days of mourning for my father are at hand,
- then will I slay my brother Jacob.

Jacob afraid & running from his father-in law

Genesis 31:31

Jacob answered and said to Laban:
- Because I was afraid, for I said, peradventure thou would take by force thy daughters from me.

<u>Jacob afraid to meet His Brother</u>

Genesis 32:7-12

Then Jacob was greatly afraid and distressed. So, he divided the people that was with him, and the flocks, and herds, and the camels, into two band.
    And said:
- If Esau come to the one company, and smite it, then the other company which is left shall escape.

And Jacob said:
- God of my father Abraham, and God of my father Isaac, the Lord which said unto me, return unto thy country, and to thy kindred, and I will deal well with thee.

- I am not worthy of the least of all the mercies, and of all the truth, which thou hast shewed unto thy servant.

- For with my staff I passed over this Jordan and now I am become two bands.

- Deliver me, I pray thee, from the hand of my brother, from the hand of Esau for I fear him, lest he come and smite me, and the mother with the children.

- Thou said, I will surely do thee good, and make thy seed as the sand of the sea, which cannot be numbered for multitude.

Jacob Wrestled with an Angel

Genesis 32:24-30

And Jacob was left alone and there wrestled a man with him until the breaking of the day. When he saw that he prevailed not against him, he touched the hollow of his thigh and the hollow of Jacob's thigh was out of joint, as he wrestled with him.

He (Angel) said,
- Let me go, for the day breaks.

He (Jacob) said,
- I will not let thee go except thou bless me.

He (Angel) said unto him, what is thy name?
- He said, Jacob.

He (Angel) said,
- Thy name shall be called no more Jacob, but Israel for as a prince hast thou power with God and with men, and hast prevailed.

Jacob asked him, and said,
- Tell me, I pray thee, thy name.

He(Angel) said,
- Wherefore is it that thou dost ask after my name?
- He (Angel) blessed him there.

Jacob called the name of the place Peniel,
for I have seen God face to face and my life is preserved.

Please answer the following questions:
- Why should God bless such a scoundrel?
- If God was with Jacob why should he be afraid of his father-in-law or brother?
- What is our takeaway from the life of Jacob and his issues with fear?

FEARS

Joseph

Most of Joseph's life was lived in fear. A naïve young boy overtaken by his jealous older brothers and sold into slavery not knowing what will happen next. Few of us even can conceive of the kind of fear he faced. Then, he faced a life either in prison or as a forced slave. His fear was what those in control might do to him. Might I add that slavery & prison in ancient days cannot be compared to todays' Holiday Inn experience called incarceration. Historical accounts show the truth of a brutal, inhuman, and unsanitary system.[xiv] His greatest fears came true when he was lied about by superiors. Throughout his experience, he lost family, comforts, and care. However,

- God took care of him.
- God developed in him humility and character.
- God blessed him in the middle of his mess.
- God used him in a mighty way.
- God finally elevated him to an honorable status and he remained humble.

When he finally had an opportunity to confront his brothers, other than slightly taking advantage of the situation.

- He realized why God placed him in the position for a purpose.

- He realized how God had blessed him because he was not bitter, angry, or seeking revenge.

I am certain he would never want to go through those early years again, but surely, he realized too that God was preparing him for a time such as this! The fear of the unknown was overtaken by the excitement of the fulfillment of God's vision. Many times, we too must go through some tuff times in our lives not realizing God is right there beside us walking us through, keeping us together, and building us up in the middle of our mess. It is not until we have come through those trying times that we see in hindsight God's hand, God's love and God's direction in our life. It is at that point that we wonder why we were so overcome with fear, worry, anxiety, or concern about the situation. We wonder why we didn't just place it all in God's hands, put feet to our prayers where we could, and then eagerly watch God move in our life. It is as we come out of those conditions or situations that we then have a ministry to others who are going through a similar thing.[xv]

> The point of the story is as follows:
> - Dependence on God will bring you through any of life's issues,
> - Confidence in God will protect you through your greatest fears,
> - Faith in God will bring out the best in you.
> - Hindsight is a great revealer of God's guiding hand in our life.

BIBLE STUDY

Joseph's Brother Realizing

Genesis 43:18

The men (brothers) were afraid because they were brought into Joseph's house. They said, because of the money that was returned in our sacks at the first time are we brought in, that he may seek occasion against us, and fall upon us, and take us for bondmen, and our asses.

Joseph & the Great Reveal

Genesis 45:1-8

Then Joseph could not refrain himself before all them that stood by him.

- He cried,
  - Cause every man to go out from me.
  - There stood no man with him,
- Joseph made himself known unto his brethren.
  - He wept aloud and the Egyptians and the house of Pharaoh heard.
- Joseph said unto his brethren, I am Joseph!
  - Doth my father yet live?
- His brethren could not answer him,
  - For they were troubled at his presence.
- Joseph said unto his brethren,
  - Come near to me, I pray you.
  - And they came near.
- He said,
  - I am Joseph your brother,
  - whom you sold into Egypt.
  - Now therefore be not grieved, nor angry with yourselves, that you sold me hither:
    - For God did send me before you to preserve life.

2 Corinthians 1:3-4

Blessed be God, even the Father of our Lord Jesus Christ, the Father of mercies, and the God of all comfort. Who comforts us in all our tribulation, that:
1. We may be able to comfort them which are in any trouble,
2. By the comfort wherewith we ourselves are comforted of God!

Please answer the following questions:
- What fear grips you right now?
- Why haven't you turn that fear over to God?
- Have you turned your fear into prayers?
- Have you put feet to your prayers where possible and left the remainder to God?

BOLAND

FEARS

Moses
& the Israelites

Moses fought several bouts with fear. This is a story of a man wanting to do good by his family and kinsman. Yet everywhere he turns, he is met with skepticism, griping, and complaining. It's times like these that make a person just want to quit and say:

"FINE! I'll just leave you alone."

He thought he was helping out those of his kind. Yet, he ended up killing a guard and being mocked by the very group he tried to protect. This eventually caused him to fear for his life and run away. With good cause I might add!

He then, encountered God in a way which changed his entire life's work. It caused him to return to his old neighborhood. It made him learn to make peace with his past before he could go on to his God given purpose. "Yes, God changed you"…that is just the kind of reaction those of us who face a life changing encounters with God can expect from those who know us best. Skeptics! Unbelievers! At first you are afraid to say anything because really, who will believe you? Then, they stay true to their form…no one believes you! After that you begin questioning yourself. Did I really change or was it just a fabrication of my imagination?

However, in this case people began believing Moses because of the proof:

- As an individual he was different,
- God showed Himself as real,
- Confrontation between Pharaoh and Moses wasn't about "personalities" it was about "the Word of God".

Isn't that what happens in our world? People only believe after you prove by the change of conduct, character, and attitude.

Then Moses got to lead God's chosen people out of Egypt. But they were no different than before: griping, belly aching, rebelling and being hard to control. Their fears were:

- First, it was the Pharaoh would get them,
- Then, it was starvation,
- After that, it was Moses was gone too long,
- Another, the giants of the Promised Land.
- It was always something else.

They only called on God when their fears brought them to their knees.

Isn't that just like us today? we never seem satisfied with life yet never consider God into the factor until we are driven to our knees by life's burdens. Consider how enlightening it would be to face the problems of the world knowing that God is in control and that everything will turn out according to his timing. I am not a fatalist by any stretch of the imagination. I know one thing, life is too short to live it in a mindset of fear, darkness, and futility. Having the understanding that God is there beside you throughout life provides a positive, uplifting and healthy outlook no matter what the circumstances.

> The point of the story is as follows:
> - With God you can face any problem,
> - With God you can overcome any obstacle,
> - With God you can reach your greatest abilities & achievements.

BIBLE STUDY

Moses & Pharaoh

Exodus 2:11-15

It came to pass in those days, when Moses was grown, that he went out unto his brethren, and looked on their burdens: and he spied an Egyptian smiting a Hebrew, one of his brethren.

- He looked this way and that way, and when he saw that there was no man, he slew the Egyptian, and hid him in the sand.
- When he went out the second day, behold, two men of the Hebrews strove together and he said to him that did the wrong:
  - Wherefore, smite thou thy fellow?
  - Who made thee a prince and a judge over us?
  - Intend to kill me, as thou killed the Egyptian?

And Moses feared, and said:
- Surely, this thing is known.

Now when Pharaoh heard this thing, he sought to slay Moses. But Moses fled from the face of Pharaoh and dwelt in the land of Midian and he sat down by a well.

<u>Moses & God</u>

Exodus 3:3-6

Now Moses kept the flock of Jethro his father in law, the priest of Midian and he led the flock to the backside of the desert and came to the mountain of God, even to Horeb.
- The angel of the Lord appeared unto him (Moses) in a flame of fire out of the midst of a bush
- He (Moses) looked, and behold, the bush burned with fire, and the bush was not consumed.
- Moses said,
  - I will now turn aside and set this great sight, why the bush is not burnt.

The Lord saw that he turned aside to see, God called unto him out of the midst of the bush, and said:

- Moses, Moses.

He (Moses) said:

- Here am I.

God said:

- Draw not nigh hither: put off thy shoes from off thy feet, for the place whereon thou stand is holy ground.
- I am the God of thy father, the God of Abraham, the god of Isaac, and the God of Jacob.

Moses hid his face for he was afraid to look upon God.

Israelites & Pharaoh

Exodus 14:10

When Pharaoh drew nigh:

- The children of Israel lifted up their eyes,
- Behold, the Egyptians marched after them,
- They were sore afraid and cried out unto the Lord.

Israelites & the Giants

Exodus 14:1, 8-9

And all the congregation lifted up their voice and cried and the people wept that night:

- If the Lord delight in us, then he will bring us into this land, and give it us.
  - A land which flows with milk and honey.

- Only rebel not against the Lord,
- Neither fear the people of the land,
    - For they are bread for us,
    - Their defense is departed from them, and the Lord is with us.
    - Fear them not!

Deuteronomy 1:28-33 (MSG)

But then you were not willing to go up. You rebelled against God, your God's plain word. You complained in your tents:
- "God hates us.
- God hauled us out of Egypt in order to dump us among the Amorites a death sentence for sure!
- How can we go up?
- We are trapped in a dead end.
- Our brothers took all the wind out of our sails, telling us,
    - 'The people are bigger and stronger than we are,
    - Their cities are huge,
    - Their defenses massive,
    - We even saw Anakite giants there!'"

I (Moses) tried to relieve your fears: "Don't be terrified of them.
- God, your God, is leading the way,
- God is fighting for you,
    - You saw with your own eyes what he did for you in Egypt,
- You saw what he did in the wilderness, how God, your God
    - Carried you as a father carries his child,

- o Carried you the whole way until you arrived here.
- But now that you are here, you won't trust God, your God,
  - o This same God who goes ahead of you in your travels to scout out a place to pitch camp, a fire by night and a cloud by day to show you the way to go."

Please answer the following questions:
- Do you not consider God until after you start having trouble?
- Do you currently face personal fears?
- Do you find yourself griping & complaining too much?
- Do you find trust in God in short supply in your life?
- So, if the answer is yes to anyone of these, what will you do about it?

BOLAND

FEARS

83

Gideon

Now is the story of Gideon, translated as Gedeon, also known as Jerubbesheth. He is described by many as a military leader, a judge, or a prophet. However, the truth is that:

- He was not an overly important person of the time.
- His tribe was one of the least important in Israel.
- When God called, he was hiding in fear in a winepress.
- When he hears that God will use him to save Israel, he does not believe it.

Gideon not only doubts his own abilities, but he also doubts the call of God on his life. He doubts it so much that he asks for proof through the dampening and drying of a fleece to prove that it was God who he was interacting with.

When he eventually does create an army, he calls up 32,000 men.[xvi] God forces him to send 22,000 home. Then God tested the remaining 10,000 by drinking which only 300 men passed. The remaining 300 men created noise with trumpets and smashing jars, which confused the Midianite camp. The Midianites ended up killing themselves.

The point of the story is as follows:

- God uses people in spite of their fears & doubts,
- God's Word guides people in spite of their background,
- God's plan is always based on faith, Success is based on trusting God's Word not man's opinion.

BIBLE STUDY

Judges 6:11-40

An angel of the Lord sat under an oak which was in Ophrah, that pertained unto Joash the Abiezrite and his son Gideon threshed wheat by the winepress, to hide it from the Midianites.

The angel of the Lord appeared unto him, and said unto him:

- The Lord is with thee, thou mighty man of valor,

And Gideon said unto him:

- Oh, my Lord if the Lord be with us, why then is all this befallen us?
- Where be all His miracles which our fathers told us of, saying, did not the Lord bring us up from Egypt?
- But now the Lord hath forsaken us and delivered us into the hands of the Midianites.

The Lord looked upon him and said:

- Go in this thy might and thou shalt save Israel from the hand of the Midianites, have not I sent thee?

He said unto him:

- Oh, my Lord, wherewith shall I save Israel?
- Behold, my family is poor in Manasseh
- I am the least in my father's house.

The Lord said unto him:

- Surely, I will be with thee,
- Thou shalt smite the Midianites as one man...

Then the angel of the Lord departed out of his sight...

The Lord said unto him:

- Peace be unto thee,
- Fear not,
- Thou shalt not die.

Then Gideon built an altar there unto the Lord and called it Jehovah shalom, unto this day it is yet in Ophrah of the Abiezrites...

The Spirit of the Lord came upon Gideon, and he blew a trumpet and Abiezer was gathered after him...

Gideon said unto God:

- If thou wilt save Israel by mine hand, as thou hast said. Behold, I will put a fleece of wool in the floor and if the dew be on the fleece only, and it be dry upon all the earth beside, then shall I know that

thou wilt save Israel by mine hand, as thou hast said.
- It was so, for he rose up early on the morrow and thrust the fleece together and ringed the dew out of the fleece, a bowl full of water.

Gideon said unto God:
- Let not thine anger be hot against me and I will speak but this once: let me prove, I pray thee but this once with the fleece. Let it now be dry only upon the fleece, and upon all the ground let there be dew.
- God did so that night, for it was dry upon the fleece only, and there was dew on all the ground.

Judges 7: 7,18-19,22

The Lord said unto Gideon,
- By the three hundred men that lapped will I save you and deliver the Midianites into thine hand: and let all the other people go every man unto his place.
- When I blow with a trumpet, I and all that are with me, then blow ye the trumpets also on every side of all the camp, and say, The sword of the Lord, and of Gideon.
- So Gideon, and the hundred men that were with him, came unto the outside of the camp in the beginning of the middle watch; and they had but newly set the watch: and they blew the trumpets, and brake the pitchers that were in their hands.

The three hundred blew the trumpets, and the Lord set every man's sword against his fellow, even throughout all the host...

Judges 8:22-23

Then the men of Israel said unto Gideon, rule thou over us, both thou, and thy son, and thy son's son also: for thou hast delivered us from the hand of Midian.

Gideon said unto them:
- I will not rule over you, neither shall my son rule over you, the Lord shall rule over you.

Please answer the following questions:
- Have you ever found yourself hiding from God's Will in your life?
- Does the idea of being used by God scare you?
- Does the idea of doing great things for God seem farfetched in your life?
- Have you ever doubted the call of God to the point you too have put out a fleece?

BOLAND

FEARS

Naomi & Ruth

This is the story of three women left husbandless in the ancient world. This had to be a frightening experience for these ladies. In the beginning the matriarch and her family were Judean refugees, who settled in Moab to escape a famine going on in Judah. Her sons married two Moabite women. Then all three men died. Obviously, after the death of the last remaining male, the women feared what might happen to them. The matriarch decided to return to Judea. The one daughter-in-law, Orpah, returned to her family. The other, named Ruth, stayed with the mother-in-law, and followed her back to her Judean community of Bethlehem. It is here, where she eventually meets and marries a man named Boaz, a distant relative of her late father-in-law. It is through this experience that she becomes the symbol of abiding loyalty and devotion. She overcame several things:

- Her fears,
- Her being an outsider in a different culture,
- Her ability to provide for herself or Naomi.

Ruth's story is celebrated during the Jewish festival of Shavuot, the Feast of Weeks, which is 50 days after Passover. Shavuot, the holiday that commemorates the Israelites receiving the Ten Commandments at Mount Sinai. It is also called the Festival of First Fruits and Grains, a fulfillment of the promise of spring. The name means "weeks", so named for the 7-week period from Passover to Shavuot.[xvii] She is remembered because of her conduct and attitude during the harvest. She is considered a celebrity because she did the right thing and acted unselfishly. Her behavior broke the rules of conformity toward her kinsman Boaz. She eventually was accepted by the Jewish people. Her status was finalized when she married Boaz, thus becoming the ancestor of King David.

> The point of the story is as follows:
> - Fear of the unknown is a natural response.
> - Overcoming fear by reliance on God is a supernatural response.
> - Dependence on God enhances supernatural outcomes.

FEARS

BIBLE STUDY

<u>Losing Husband</u>

Ruth 1:14-16

They lifted up their voice and wept again:
- Orpah kissed her mother-in-law,
- Ruth clave unto her.

And she (Naomi) said:
- Behold, thy sister in law is gone back unto her people, and unto her gods, return thou (Ruth) after thy sister in law.

Ruth said:
- Intreat me not to leave thee, or to return from following after thee.
- For whither thou go, I will go,
- Where thou lodge, I will lodge,
- Thy people shall be my people,
- Thy God my God:

Ruth 3:10-12

He (Boaz) said (to Ruth):
- Blessed be thou of the Lord, my daughter,
- For thou hast shewed more kindness in the latter end than at the beginning, inasmuch as thou followed not young men, whether poor or rich.
- Now, my daughter fear not,
- I will do to thee all that thou require,
- For all the city of my people doth know that thou art a virtuous woman.

- Now it is true that I am thy near kinsman, howbeit there is a kinsman nearer than I.

Please answer the following questions:
- Why do you think Ruth did not go back to her own people in her time of need?
- What overcame her fears?
  - Belief in God
  - Her conduct?
  - Boaz attitude?
  - Explain your answer.

BOLAND

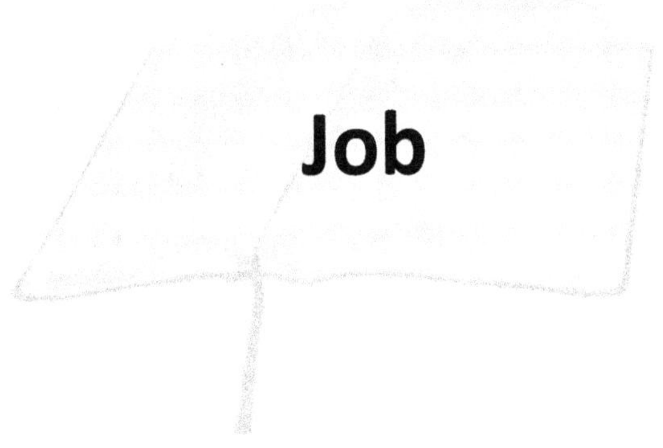Job

Things could not have gotten any better for this wealthy individual, yet in a short series of events things got very, very bad. In a short but catastrophic series of events Job loses his livestock, servants, and children to thieves, trespassers, & natural catastrophes. Job then suffers from skin sores and is banished from his home and village. Job's wife becomes the voice of discouragement and campaigns for him to curse God, give up, and die. Job refuses & struggles on in his circumstances.

Eventually three so-called friends come to visit him in his misery. At first, they all sit in silence for seven days out of respect for his mourning. But eventually, they speak:

- He is accused of committing some sin and urged to confess & seek God's favor.
- His children are accused of bringing on their deaths by their own conduct.
- He is accused of deserving greater punishment than what he has received.
- He is accused of spending too much energy justifying himself rather than giving God glory & honor.
- He is accused of excessive talking, which could be considered rebellion against God.

It was said that God converses with humans through visions and physical pain. One young friend of Job's showed up at the end with the attitude that he knew the mind of and could speak for God. He had the attitude that he knew better than his elders. God finally interrupted the human conversation, admonished Job's friends for insulting both Job and their lack of knowledge about the God of creation. He then called upon Job to be brave. God set a series of questions before him. God's questions intending to show how little humankind knows about creation and how much power God alone has! His circumstances humbled Job as it would humble any of us.

The point of the story is as follows:
- Pain & suffering are not to be feared if God is with us.
- Pain & suffering are not always a result of sin!
- Pain & suffering open up doors of ministry to others who suffer in similar ways.
- Sometimes it is best if "real friends" say nothing when friends are suffering. Just be there!

BIBLE STUDY

<u>Job's Troubles</u>

Job 3:25
- The thing which I greatly feared is come upon me,
- That which I was afraid of is come unto me.

Job 4:6
- Is not this thy fear, thy confidence, thy hope, and the uprightness of thy ways?

Job 4:14
- Fear came upon me, and trembling, which made all my bones to shake.

Job 6:14
- To him that is afflicted pity should be showed from his friend,
- But he forsakes the fear of the Almighty.

Please answer the following questions:
- What is (or was) your greatest fear?
- How would (or did) you overcome it?
  - Have you been able to minister to others with that same fear?
  - Why or why not?

FEARS

Elijah

Elijah's greatest fear came after his greatest victory??? He had restored life to the widow's dead child. He had just wiped out the prophets of Baal, who supported the evil Jezebel. He had showed the Israelites that God was who He said He was. Now, just because the queen puts out a death threat against him, he runs for his life! So, what was the reality of the moment?

- God told him that He was on his side.
- God told him that he would not die.
- God told him that He would protect him.
- God showed up at Mount Carmel.

Yet, all that did not seem to matter when the queen, a mere mortal, threatens physical violence. Isn't that the way we are too? We read God's Word and claim the promises of safety, protection and to provision. Yet, we are either not convinced, or have a failure of belief in our time of anxiety. Just as Elijah had!

The point of the story is as follows:
- The Word of God promises personal safety, protection & provision.
- Trust in God's Word banishes a lack of faith.
- Worry is assuming responsibilities God never intended us to have.

BOLAND

BIBLE STUDY

<u>Elijah vs. Baal's Prophets</u>

1 Kings 18:22-24

Then said Elijah unto the people,
- I, even I only, remain a prophet of the Lord
- Baal's prophets are four hundred and fifty men.

Therefore, give us two bullocks
- Let them (Baal's prophet's) choose one bullock for themselves,
  - Cut it in pieces, and lay it on wood, and put no fire under
  - Call on the name of your gods.
- I will dress the other bullock,
  - Lay it on wood and put no fire under.
  - I will call on the name of the Lord.
- The God that answers by fire, let him be God.

All the people answered and said:
- It is well spoken.

<u>Baal's Big Failure</u>

1 King 18 26-29

They (Baal's Prophet's) took the bullock, which was given them, they dressed it. They called on the name of Baal from morning even until noon, saying:

- O Baal, hear us.

But there was no voice, nor any that answered.
They leaped upon the altar which was made. It came to pass at noon, that Elijah mocked them, and said, cry aloud:

- He is a god?
- Is he talking?
- Is he pursuing?
- Is he on a journey?
- Is he asleep and must be awaken?

Then:

- They cried aloud!
- They cut themselves after their manner with knives and lancets, till the blood gushed out upon them!

It came to pass, when midday was past:

- They prophesied until the time of the offering of the evening sacrifice,
- There was neither voice, nor any to answer, nor any that regarded.

<u>God's Big Reveal</u>

1 King 18 30-36

Elijah said unto all the people:
Come near unto me
- He repaired the altar of the Lord that was broken down.
- Elijah took twelve stones,
- according to the number of the tribes of the sons of Jacob, unto whom the Word of the Lord came, saying, Israel shall be thy name.
- With the stones he built an altar in the name of the Lord
- He made a trench about the altar, as great as would contain two measures of seed.
- He put the wood in order,
- He cut the bullock in pieces,
- He laid him on the wood,

He said,
- Fill four barrels with water, and
  - pour it on the burnt sacrifice,
  - and on the wood.

He said:
- Do it the second time.
  - And they did it the second time.

He said,
- Do it the third time.
  - And they did it the third time.
- The water ran round about the altar
- He filled the trench also with water.

It came to pass at the time of the offering of the evening sacrifice, Elijah the prophet came near, and said:

- Lord God of Abraham, Isaac, and of Israel, let it be known this day that thou art God in Israel, and
  - o   I am Thy servant,
  - o   I have done all these things at Thy Word.
- Hear me, O Lord, hear me, that this people may know that thou art the Lord God, and that thou hast turned their heart back again.
- Then the fire of the Lord fell,
  - o   Consumed the burnt sacrifice,
  - o   Consumed the wood,
  - o   Consumed the stones,
  - o   Consumed the dust,
  - o   Licked up the water that was in the trench.

<u>The killing of Baal's prophets</u>

1 King 18: 40

Elijah said unto them:
- Take the prophets of Baal,
- Let not one of them escape.
- They (the people) took them,
- Elijah brought them down to the brook Kishon and slew them there.

<u>Jezebel vs. Elijah</u>

1 Kings 19:1-4

And Ahab told Jezebel all that Elijah had done, and
1. How he had slain all the prophets with the sword.
2. Then Jezebel sent a messenger unto Elijah, saying,
    a. So, let the gods do to me, and more also, if I make not thy life as the life of one of them by tomorrow about this time.
3. And when he saw that he (Elijah) arose, and went for his life,

[When he] came to Beersheba, which belongs to Judah, and left his servant there. But he himself went a day's journey into the wilderness, and came and sat down under a juniper tree: and
- He (Elijah) requested for himself that he might die, and said,
    o   It is enough now, O Lord, take away my life,
    o   For I am not better than my fathers.

Please answer the following questions:
- Why do we ever doubt God's Word?
- Why is it so hard, when in the middle of our battles to remember the Word of God?
- Why is it that when worries hit we focus on mankind rather than relying on God?

FEARS

King Saul

Saul is a sad character in Scripture. The people wanted a king like everyone else had. Yet, when God chose Saul:

- He did not want it.
- He was afraid.
- He hid himself.
- The people dragged him out of hiding.
- Some did not like God's choice.
- God anointed him king anyway.

Then God directed him on an assignment. His orders were to go kill the king of the Amalekites and utterly destroy everything they own. Simple and direct orders!

Unfortunately, Saul failed, he couldn't obey a direct order. He claimed he was afraid of the people so he let things get out of hand. They returned with the king of the Amalekites as a prisoner and the spoils of war. Saul claimed it was to sacrifice to the Lord, but the prophet Samuel knew better. Samuel intercepted Saul. Saul through the people under the bus by blaming them for the decision to take things and spare the king. Samuel killed Agag the king and declared God unhappy with Saul as king.

This was just the beginning of Saul's personal troubles!

The point of the story is as follows:
- We should fear God's Word more than man's advice!
- Disobedience to God's Word comes with consequences!
- When we are given or accept a personal responsibility, we are not to blame others for failures and shortcomings.

BIBLE STUDY

<u>The Choosing of the King</u>

1 Samuel 10:20-2

Then Samuel brought:
- All the tribes of Israel near,
- The tribe of Benjamin was taken by lot,
- The tribe of Benjamin nearby its clans,
- The clan of the Matrites was taken by lot,
- Saul the son of Kish was taken by lot,
  - But when they sought him,
  - He could not be found.

So, they inquired again of the Lord,
- "Is there a man still to come?"

The Lord said:
- "Behold, he has hidden himself among the baggage."
  Then they ran and took him from there.

<u>Hometown reaction</u>

1 Samuel 10: 26-27

Saul also went to his home at Gibeah, and with him went men of valor whose hearts God had touched.

Some worthless fellows said:
- "How can this man save us?"

They despised him,
- brought him no present,

- They held his peace.

God's Instructions to Saul

1 Samuel 15:1-3

Samuel also said unto Saul:
- The Lord sent me to anoint thee to be king over his people, over Israel.
- Now therefore hearken thou unto the voice of the words of the Lord. Thus, saith the Lord of hosts:
  - I remember that which Amalek did to Israel,
  - How he laid wait for him in the way when he came up from Egypt.
  - Now go and smite Amalek:
    - Utterly destroy all that they have...
    - Spare them not...
    - Slay both man and woman, infant and suckling, ox and sheep, camel, and ass.

His Sin

1 Samuel 15:9

Saul and the people:
- Spared Agag,
- He spared the best of the sheep, of the oxen, of the fatlings, of the lambs, and all that was good, and would not utterly destroy them.
- Everything that was vile and refuse they destroyed utterly.

Saul's Defense

1 Samuel 15:20-21

Saul said unto Samuel:
- Yea, <u>I have obeyed</u> the voice of the Lord, and have gone the way which the Lord sent me, and have brought Agag the king of Amalek, and have utterly destroyed the Amalekites.
- <u>But</u> the people took of the spoil, sheep and oxen, the chief of the things which should have been utterly destroyed, to sacrifice unto the Lord thy God in Gilgal.

God's Response

1 Samuel 15:22-23

Samuel said,
- Hath the Lord as great delight in burnt offerings and sacrifices, as in obeying the voice of the Lord?
- Behold, to obey is better than sacrifice, and to hearken than the fat of rams.
- For <u>rebellion</u> is as the sin of witchcraft, and <u>stubbornness</u> is as iniquity and idolatry.
- Because thou hast rejected the word of the Lord, he hath also rejected thee from being king

Saul's Confession

1 Samuel 15:24

And Saul said unto Samuel:
- I have sinned, for I have transgressed the commandment of the Lord and thy words:
  - Because I feared the people and obeyed their voice.

God's Final Answer

1 Samuel 15:32-33

Then said Samuel:
- Bring hither to me Agag the king of the Amalekites.
  - Agag came unto him delicately.

Agag said,
- Surely the bitterness of death is past.

Samuel said:
- As thy sword hath made women childless,
- So shall thy mother be childless among women.
- And Samuel hewed Agag in pieces before the Lord in Gilgal.

Please answer the following questions:

- Why are we afraid to accept responsibility for our decisions good or bad?
- Why is it so easy to blame others for our short falls & failures?
- Why is it so hard to be honest with God?

FEARS

King David

Consider this man after God's own heart. The killer of lions, bears, & Goliath. What could he possibly be afraid of? Well, it seems many things:

- He was afraid of Saul who tried to kill him on several occasions.
  - He ran away and hid from him.
  - He hid wherever he could in caves, with crooks or in a cranny.
- He was afraid of King Achish who became aware of his reputation and plotted against him.
  - He changed his behavior and pretended to be insane so he could escape.
- He was afraid of God when the men moving the Ark of the covenant were struck dead.
  - He left the Ark in haste,
  - Yet God blessed the person caring for it.
- He was afraid of the angel where he had sacrificed in order to stop the plague.
  - He then began gathering material to build the temple.

The point of the story is as follows:
- God's Word protects us from our fears.
- Changing our behavior to hide our fears is pointless.
- Running from our fears rather than facing them works for only so long.

BOLAND

BIBLE STUDY

<u>David's Fears</u>

1 Samuel 21:10

David arose and fled that day for fear of Saul and went to Achish the king of Gath.

1 Samuel 21:11-13

The servants of Achish said:
- Is not this David the king of the land?
- Did they not sing to one another of him in dance?
    "Saul has struck down his thousands,
        and David his ten thousands'?"
- David took these words to heart and
- He was much afraid of Achish the king of Gath.
- He changed his behavior before them:
    - Pretended to be insane in their hands,
    - Made marks on the doors of the gate ,
    - Let his spittle run down his beard.

1 Samuel 22:1

- David departed from there and escaped to the cave of Adullam

2 Samuel 6:1-11

David again gathered thirty thousand men of Israel.
- David arose and went to bring up from there the ark of God,
- They carried the ark of God on a new cart and Uzzah and Ahio, were driving the new cart, with the ark of God on it...
- When they came to the threshing floor of Nacon,
  - Uzzah put out his hand to the ark of God and took hold of it, for the oxen stumbled.
  - The anger of the Lord was kindled against Uzzah,
  - God struck him down there because of his error, and he died there beside the ark of God.
- David was angry because the Lord had broken out against Uzzah.
- David was afraid of the Lord that day, and he said:
  - How can the ark of the Lord come to me?
- David was not willing to take the ark of the Lord into the city of David.
- David took it aside to the house of Obed-Edom the Gittite.
  - The ark of the Lord remained in the house of Obed-Edom the Gittite three months.
  - The Lord blessed Obed-Edom and all his household.

1 Chronicles 21:28-30

At that time when David saw that the Lord had answered him at the threshing floor…
- He sacrificed there.

For the tabernacle of the Lord, which Moses had made in the wilderness, and the altar of burnt offering were at that time in the high place at Gibeon,
- David could not go before it to inquire of God,
- He was afraid of the sword of the angel of the Lord.

Psalm 27:1
- The Lord is my light and my salvation,
  - Whom shall, I fear?
- The Lord is the stronghold of my life,
  - Whom shall I be afraid?

Please answer the following questions:
- Was David justified in running from fear?
- What would have been the best thing for David to do in dealing with fear?
- Does knowing how David dealt with fear help us today?
- In reading Psalm 27, why didn't David take his own advice?

FEARS

Jeremiah

God used Jeremiah in a mighty way to warn the Israelites of their coming calamity and doom.

Jeremiah responding to God's call:
- Put up excuses,
- Expressed his fear.

The Israelites:
- Did not want to hear God's Word,
- They tried:
  - To ignore it,
  - To hide it,
  - To kill it,
  - To imprison it,
- They responded by:
  - Ignoring the obvious reality,
  - Replacing it with the politically correct reality, of their own making.
- Unfortunately for them,
  - Nothing can, could or would hinder the revealed Will of God.

Jeremiah was, at first, afraid because he felt that he was too young.

- He later was concerned for his life because of how the others treated him.
- It seems it would have been better for him to just go along with the good news rather than declare the truth.

Consider our culture today. It seems we are similar to Israel of Jeremiah's day.

The cultural church of today:
- Makes worship an event.
- Creates a politically correct bible,
  - To suit & justify its lifestyle.

The culture church today forgot that:
- God's (original) Word has not changed.
- God's (original) Warnings are still in effect.
- Disobedience to God's Word still carries with it, dire consequences.
- Decisions have consequences!

The point of the story is as follows:
- Fear is no obstacle when being used by God.
- Fear is overcome when God is in control.
- Fear tries to limit the power of God,
  His ability, His Word, & His chosen,
  for His Glory & Honor.

FEARS

BIBLE STUDY

<u>God to Jeremiah</u>

Jeremiah 1: 4-8

Then the word of the Lord came unto me (Jeremiah) saying:
- Before I formed thee in the belly,
  - I knew thee
- Before thou came forth out of the womb,
  - I sanctified thee,
- I ordained thee a prophet unto the nations.

Then said I:
- Ah, Lord God! behold, I cannot speak, for I am a child.

But the Lord said unto me:
- Say not, I am a child,
  - Thou shalt go to all that I shall send thee.
- Whatsoever I command thee
  - Thou shalt speak.
- Be not afraid of their faces,
  - I am with thee to deliver thee, saith the Lord.

<u>Prophecy vs. Abuse</u>

Jeremiah 18:17-19, 23

- I (God) will scatter them (Israelites) as with an east wind before the enemy.
- I will show them the back, and not the face, in the day of their calamity.

Then said they (Jerusalem leaders),
- Come and let us devise devices against Jeremiah for the law shall not perish from the priest, nor counsel from the wise, nor the word from the prophet.
- Come, and let us smite him with the tongue, and let us not give heed to any of his words.

Give heed to me (Jeremiah), O Lord, and hearken to the voice of them that contend with me.

Jeremiah's Response:
- Lord, thou know all their counsel against me to slay me,
- Forgive not their iniquity,
- Neither blot out their sin from thy sight,
- Let them be overthrown before thee,
- Deal thus with them in the time of thine anger.

Jeremiah 20:1-2, 7

Now Pashur the priest, who was also chief governor in the house of the Lord, heard that Jeremiah prophesied these things.

- Then Pashur smote (hit hard) Jeremiah the prophet and put him in the stocks …

Jeremiah's Response:

- Lord, thou hast deceived me, and I was deceived,
- thou art stronger than I, and hast prevailed,
- I am in derision daily, everyone mocks me.

Jeremiah 26:8-9

Now it came to pass, when Jeremiah had made an end of speaking all that the Lord had commanded him to speak unto all the people, that the priests and the prophets and all the people took him, saying:

- Thou shalt surely die.

Why hast thou prophesied in the name of the Lord, saying:

- This house shall be like Shiloh,
- This city shall be desolate without an inhabitant?

And all the people were gathered against Jeremiah in the house of the Lord.

Jeremiah 26:20-24

There was also a man that prophesied in the name of the Lord, Urijah the son of Shemaiah of Kirjathjearim,

- He prophesied against this city and against this land according to all the words of Jeremiah.
- King Jehoiakim, with all his warriors and all the officials, heard his words, the king sought to put him to death.
    - o When Uriah heard of it, he was afraid and fled and escaped to Egypt.

King Jehoiakim sent to Egypt certain men…and they took Uriah from Egypt and brought him to King Jehoiakim,

- Who struck him down with the sword,
- Dumped his dead body into the burial place of the common people!
- The hand of Ahikam, the royal secretary, was with Jeremiah,
    - o That they should not give him into the hand of the people to put him to death.

Jeremiah 37:13-16

When he was in the gate of Benjamin, a captain of the ward was there, whose name was Irijah and he took Jeremiah the prophet, saying,

- Thou fall away to the Chaldeans.
  Then said Jeremiah,
- It is false,
- I fall not away to the Chaldeans.
- But he harkened not to him,
- Irijah took Jeremiah and brought him to the princes.

Wherefore the princes were wroth (angry) with Jeremiah,

- They Smote (hit hard) him,
- Put him in prison...
- When Jeremiah was entered into the dungeon,
- Jeremiah had remained there many days.

Jeremiah 37:21

Then Zedekiah the king commanded that they should commit Jeremiah into the court of the prison, and that they should give him daily a piece of bread out of the bakers' street, until all the bread in the city were spent.

- Thus, Jeremiah remained in the court of the prison.

Jeremiah 38:6, 10, 28
- Then took they Jeremiah,
- Cast him into the dungeon...that was in the court of the prison,
- They let down Jeremiah with cords,
- In the dungeon there was no water, but mire:
    - Jeremiah sunk in the mire.

Then the king commanded Ebedmelech the Ethiopian, saying:
- Take from hence thirty men with thee,
- Take up Jeremiah the prophet out of the dungeon before he dies.
- Jeremiah abode in the court of the prison until the day that Jerusalem was taken,
- he (Jeremiah) was there when Jerusalem was taken.

Please answer the following questions:

- Why is it so hard when things go wrong in our life, to remember the promises of God?
- What is one take away from the experiences of Jeremiah?

BOLAND

Daniel

A young man, taken from his family, turned into a eunuch, learned a new language, trained to serve his enemy's leader, yet continued to worship his God. No one today can imagine how frightened he must have been in those early days of his captivity. Yet, he continued to have faith in God. He stayed true to his convictions even:

- In the face of God sized issues,
- The threat of torture,
- The realization of humiliation,
- The possibility of death.

God pursued him, used him, and honored him throughout his life.

It had to be extremely difficult to be a God faithful individual in an atheistic world at the time of Daniel. The threat to compromise his faith had to be all around him. Would any modern-day believer stand up for the God of Creation knowing that personal threats, torture or even death were the possibilities being offered for dissention by a secular world?

> The point of the story is as follows:
> - God uses individuals no matter what!
> - God doesn't abandon true believers to their fears.
> - True believers are rewarded and protected in their faithfulness.

BIBLE STUDY

<u>Daniel's Request</u>

<u>Daniel 1:8</u>

But Daniel purposed in his heart that he would not defile himself:
- With the portion of the king's meat,
- With the wine which he drank.

Therefore, he requested of the prince of the eunuchs that he might not defile himself.
- Now God had brought Daniel into favor and tender love with the prince of the eunuchs.

The prince of the eunuchs said unto Daniel:
- I fear my lord the king,
- Who hath appointed your meat and your drink!
- Why should he see your faces worse liking than the children which are of your sort?
- Then shall ye make me endanger my head to the king.

Encounter with the Angel

Daniel 10: 4-8 (MSG)

"On the twenty-fourth day of the first month I was standing on the bank of the great river, the Tigris.
1. I looked up and to my surprise saw a man dressed in linen with a belt of pure gold around his waist.
    a. His body was hard and glistening, as if sculpted from a precious stone,
    b. His face radiant,
    c. his eyes bright and penetrating like torches,
    d. his arms and feet glistening like polished bronze,
    e. his voice, deep and resonant, sounded like a huge choir of voices.

2. "I, Daniel, was the only one to see this. The men who were with me, although they did not see it,
    a. were overcome with fear and ran off and hid, <u>fearing</u> the worst. Left alone after the appearance, abandoned by my friends, I <u>went weak</u> in the knees, the blood drained from my face.

The Lion's Den

Daniel 6:10-11

Now when Daniel knew that the writing was signed, he went into his house and his windows being open in his chamber toward Jerusalem:
- He kneeled…three times a day,
- He prayed,
- He gave thanks before his God,
  - as he did aforetime.

Then these men assembled:
- Found Daniel praying and
- Making supplication before his God.

The Consequences

Daniel 6:16-17

Then the king commanded:
- They brought Daniel,
- They cast him into the den of lions.

Now the king spoke and said unto Daniel:
- Thy God whom thou serve continually,
- He will deliver thee.

A stone was brought:
- Laid upon the mouth of the den
- The king sealed it with his own signet,
  - with the signet of his lords,
  - that the purpose might not be changed concerning Daniel.

<u>The Result</u>
Daniel 6:19-24
The king arose very early in the morning and went in haste unto the den of lions. When he came to the den, he cried with a lamentable voice unto Daniel:
- Daniel, servant of the living God,
- Is thy God, whom thou serve continually, able to deliver thee from the lions?

Then said Daniel unto the king:
- O king, live forever.
- My God
  - Hath sent his angel, and
  - Hath shut the lions' mouths,
  - That they have not hurt me: forasmuch as before him innocence was found in me,
  - Also, before thee,
    - O king, have I done no hurt!

The king commanded:
- They brought those men which had accused Daniel,
- They cast them into the den of lions,
  - Them, their children, and their wives.
  - The lions had the mastery of them,
  - Broke all their bones in pieces or ever they came at the bottom of the den.

Please answer the following questions:
- What crisis of faith do you face?
- Would you be willing to speak of for God in the face of these type threats?

BOLAND

FEARS

Shadrach, Meshach, & Abednego

Just like Daniel, his three young friends were taken from their families, castrated, retrained to serve their enemy, and tormented into believing a religious lie.

- They stood up for their convictions.
- They did not back down from their faith.
- They were not afraid to go public with their beliefs.

In declaring their beliefs publicly, they understood there would be consequences. Certainly, fear overcame them at times but they fought through the moments. They were more than willing to face these challenges. Whether or not God saved them from the outcomes of their actions. They still had faith in God!

The point of the story is as follows:
- Faith is not dependent on outcome.
- Faith is not dictated by fear.
- Faith is not based on politics.
- Faith is centered on Biblical truth & fact.

BIBLE STUDY

<u>The Fiery Furnace</u>

Daniel 3: 13-26

Then Nebuchadnezzar in his rage and fury commanded:
- To bring Shadrach, Meshach, and Abednego.
    - They brought these men before the king.

Nebuchadnezzar spoke and said unto them:
- Is it true?
    - Do not you serve my gods,
    - Nor worship the golden image
        - Which I have set up?
    - Now if you be ready that at what time you hear the sound of the cornet, flute, harp, sackbut, psaltery, and dulcimer, and all kinds of music,
        - You fall down and worship the image which I have made,
        - If you worship not, you shall be cast the same hour into the midst of a burning fiery furnace.
- Who is that God that shall deliver you out of my hands?

Shadrach, Meshach, and Abednego, answered:
- We are not careful to answer thee in this matter.
- If it be so,
  - Our God, whom we serve is able to deliver us from the burning fiery furnace.
  - He will deliver us out of thine hand.
- If not,
  - Be it known unto thee, O king,
  - That we will not serve thy gods,
  - Nor worship the golden image which thou hast set up.

Nebuchadnezzar full of fury, and the form of his visage was changed against Shadrach, Meshach, and Abednego. Therefore, he spoke, and commanded:
- They should heat the furnace one seven times more than it was wont to be heated.
- He commanded the most mighty men that were in his army to bind Shadrach, Meshach, and Abednego, and to cast them into the burning fiery furnace.
- These men were bound in their coats, their hosen, and their hats, and their other garments, and were cast into the midst of the burning fiery furnace.
- Because the king's commandment was urgent, and the furnace exceeding hot,
  - The flames of the fire slew those men that took up Shadrach, Meshach, and Abednego.
- The three men, Shadrach, Meshach, and Abednego, fell down bound into the midst of the burning fiery furnace.

Then Nebuchadnezzar the king was astonished, and rose up in haste, and spoke, and said unto his counsellors:

- Did not we cast three men bound into the midst of the fire?

They answered and said:

- True, O king.

He answered and said, Lo,

- I see four men loose, walking in the midst of the fire,
- They have no hurt,
- The form of the fourth is like the Son of God.

Then Nebuchadnezzar came near to the mouth of the burning fiery furnace, and spoke, and said:

- Shadrach, Meshach, and Abednego, you servants of the most high God, come forth, and come hither.
- Then Shadrach, Meshach, and Abednego, came forth of the midst of the fire.

Please answer the following questions:

- When was the last time you stood your ground for Christ?
- Would you stand up for your faith if it meant severe punishment?

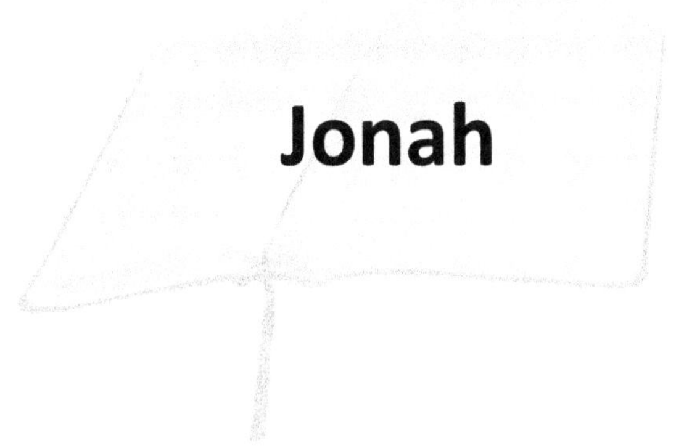

Jonah

In order to understand the Book of Jonah one must understand the history of the time. Nineveh was a city situated on the east bank of the Tigris River where sits the current city of Mosul, Iraq. It is extremely hard for those of us in today's world to really understand how much the people of the ancient world hated the Ninevites. Theirs was a hatred, disgust, animosity, revulsion. They despised this civilization with such a loathsomeness we cannot even imagine. The rulers of this civilization had the reputation of total cruelty over the people they conquered. Most history books find it too disgusting to even speak about. They were known for everything from heavy tribute, overwhelming conquest of other civilizations, to merciless treatment of conquered soldiers & leaders. They decapitated, disfigured, impaled, and did other unspeakable things to soldiers and civilians alike.

Now, with that in mind, here is the prophet of God who was given a direct order from God to go to Nineveh and preach salvation to its people. However, Jonah did not like it, so he thought he could run from it! In his attempt to run from God's Will he ended up being thrown overboard by the sailors of the ship he was on and swallowed into the belly of a large fish.

- He still ended up doing God's Will, anyway.
- The city of Nineveh repented anyway, in spite of Jonah's best efforts.
- God withdrew His plan to punishment the people.
- And apparently Jonah wasn't too happy over God's decision to go easy on them either.

The point of the story is as follows:
- We should never fear God's revealed Will.
- Running from God's Will is not an option.
- God's Plans aren't necessarily our plans.
- God's Plans always succeed.
- God's Directions are not optional

BIBLE STUDY

<u>Jonah's orders</u>

Jonah 1:1-2

Now the word of the Lord came unto Jonah the son of Amittai, saying:
- Arise, go to Nineveh, that great city,
- Cry against it,
  - For their wickedness is come up before Me.

<u>Jonah's Response</u>

Jonah 1:3

Jonah rose up to flee:
- Unto Tarshish from the presence of the Lord,
  - Went down to Joppa,
- He found a ship going to Tarshish,
  - So, he paid the fare thereof,
  - Went down into it, to go with them unto Tarshish from the presence of the Lord.

<u>God's Response</u>

Jonah 1:4
- The Lord sent out a great wind into the sea,
- There was a mighty tempest in the sea,
- So, that the ship was like to be broken.

The Sailor's Response

Jonah 1:10, 15-16

Then were the men exceedingly afraid, and said unto him:
- Why hast thou done this?
- For the men knew that he fled from the presence of the Lord,
  - Because he had told them.
- So, they took up Jonah,
  - Cast him forth into the sea,
  - The sea ceased from her raging.
- Then the men feared the Lord exceedingly,
  - Offered a sacrifice unto the Lord,
  - Made vows

The Whale

Jonah 1:16, 2:7,10

Now the Lord had prepared a great fish to swallow up Jonah.
- Jonah was in the belly of the fish three days and three nights.

When my soul <u>fainted</u> within me, I remembered the Lord:
- My prayer came in unto thee, into thine holy temple.

And the Lord spoke unto the fish,
- It vomited out Jonah upon the dry land.

<u>Nineveh's Response</u>

Jonah 3:10

God saw their (Ninevites) works:
- They turned from their evil way,

God repented of the evil, that he had said that he would do unto them:
- He did it not.

Please answer the following questions:
- Know anybody running from the revealed Will of God?
- Do you realize that our will is not necessarily God's Will!
- In looking at your life, are you being swallowed up by problems.
  - Could you be running from God?

BOLAND

FEARS

Queen Esther

Queen Esther of Persia, rose from a simple Jewish girl to the wife of the biblical character King Ahasuerus, better known to historians as Xerxes the Great, c. 519 – 465 b.c. Her uncle Mordecai had an enemy in high places who had a personal vendetta against him but did not realize that she was related. They conned the king into declaring all Jews a threat to the country and issued a royal decree ordering their destruction. Mordecai gets word to Esther, who, although fearful and at the risk of her own life intervenes, exposes the plot, and causes the conspiracy to backfire on the enemies of the Jews.

The point of the story is as follows:
- Sometimes we are placed in locations and/or positions for God's purpose.
- Prayer overcomes fear.
- When in doubt about your situation or anything, pray!

BIBLE STUDY

<u>Before the King</u>

Esther 4:9-17

Hatach came and told Esther the words of Mordecai. Again, Esther spoke unto Hatach, and gave him commandment unto Mordecai,

- All the king's servants, and the people of the king's provinces, do know,
  - o Whosoever, whether man or women,
  - o Shall come unto the king into the inner court,
    - Who is not called,
  - o There is one law of his to put him to death,
  - o Except such to whom the king shall hold out the golden scepter, that he may live.
- I have not been called to come in unto the king these thirty days.

They told to Mordecai Esther's words:

Then Mordecai commanded to answer Esther:
- Think not with thyself that thou shalt escape in the king's house, more than all the Jews.
- For if thou altogether hold thy peace at this time, then shall their enlargement and deliverance arise to the Jews from another place.
- Thou and thy father's house shall be destroyed,
- Who knows whether thou art come to the kingdom for such a time as this?

Then Esther bade them return Mordecai this answer:
- Go, gather together all the Jews that are present in Shushan,
- Fast for me,
  - Neither eat nor drink three days, night or day,
  - I also and my maidens will fast likewise,
- So, will I go in unto the king,
  - Which is not according to the law,
  - If I perish, I perish.

So, Mordecai went his way,
- He did according to all that Esther had commanded him.

Please answer the following questions:
- How fearful would it be to know that by taking a position of something could cost you your life?
  - Could you do that?

FEARS

175

John the Baptist

God orchestrated the birth, ministry, and life of John the Baptist. Baptism was common among the Jewish community. So, everyone who went out to where John was knew exactly what they were doing. We have written historical evidence of ritual immersion going on prior to the advent of Christianity.[xviii]

In Jewish society water baptism is called a mikva'ot (mikvehs). This form of immersion is both for ritual and purity purposes. Even pagan religions picked up on the idea of baptism. The basic idea is to make oneself pure in order to go in the presence of a deity. It was Jewish law that requires (even to this day) one to immerse in a mikveh as part of the process of conversion, getting married, or menstrual purity or some special life event.[xix]

John declared to those doing this that he was only baptizing with water but the Messiah was coming and He would baptize with the Holy Spirit. His baptism of Jesus in the manner of "Mikveh" was the purification of the beginning of Jesus unique ministry. God's hand in the life of John was unique. Just as it was in the life of his parents and everyone around him.

- John's parents met the news of his birth with fear and uncertainty due to their age.
- The Pharisees and Sadducees met the news of John's ministry with concern because they feared they might lose power and influence over the people.
- Herod met the news of John's preaching with fear because of being condemned over the relationship he had with his brother's wife.
  - Herod was also afraid to kill John due to the loyalty of those who followed John.

The point of the story is as follows:
- Don't be afraid of doing God's revealed Will.
- God gives us assurances of His Will for our lives.
- Life is short, do not be afraid of doing God's Will as you know it.

BIBLE STUDY

<u>Zacharias the father of John the Baptist</u>

Luke 1:8-12 (MSG)

It so happened that as Zachariah was carrying out his priestly duties before God, working the shift assigned to his regiment, it came his one turn in life to enter the sanctuary of God and burn incense. The congregation was gathered and praying outside the Temple at the hour of the incense offering. Unannounced, an angel of God appeared just to the right of the altar of incense. Zachariah was paralyzed in fear.

Luke 1:12-13

And when Zacharias saw him (the angel). He was troubled, and fear fell upon him. But the angel said unto him:

- Fear not, Zacharias,
- For thy prayer is heard
- Thy wife Elisabeth shall bear thee a son,
- Thou shalt call his name John.

<u>The Birth of John</u>

Luke 1:57-66

When Elizabeth was full-term in her pregnancy, she bore a son. Her neighbors and relatives, seeing that God had overwhelmed her with mercy, celebrated with her.

On the eighth day, they came to circumcise the child and were calling him Zachariah after his father.

- His mother intervened:
  - "No. He is to be called John."

They said:
- "But no one in your family is named that."
- They used sign language to ask Zachariah what he wanted him named.

Asking for a tablet, Zachariah wrote:
- "His name is to be John."
- That took everyone by surprise.

Surprise followed surprise! Zachariah's mouth was now open, his tongue loose, and he was talking, praising God!

 A deep, reverential fear settled over the neighborhood, and in all that Judean hill country people talked about nothing else. Everyone who heard about it took it to heart, wondering:
- "What will become of this child? Clearly, God has his hand in this."

<u>Herod's fear of John the Baptist</u>

Mark 6:19-20

Therefore, Herodias had a quarrel against him (John), and would have killed him but she could not. Herod feared John, knowing that he was a just man, holy,
- Herod observed him,
- Herod heard him,

- Herod saw him do many things,
- Herod heard him gladly.

Matthew 14:3, 5, 6-9

Herod had laid hold on John, and bound him, and put him in prison
- For Herodias' sake, his brother Philip's wife.
- He (Herod) would have put him (John) to death,
- He feared the multitude because they counted him (John) as a prophet.

When Herod's birthday was kept, the daughter of Herodias danced before them, and pleased Herod.
- Whereupon he promised with an oath to give her whatsoever she would ask.
  - She, being before instructed of her mother, said:
    - Give me here John Baptist's head in a charger.
- The king was sorry:
  - Nevertheless, for the oath's sake,
  - Them which sat with him at meat,
  - He commanded it to be given her.

Please answer the following questions:
- Why do people fear the direction of God?
  - As Zachariah's family did?
- Why do people fear those who are truly being used by God?
  - As Herod did?

BOLAND

FEARS

Joseph & Mary

This is another one of those, who can even imagine the fear stories. It is ancient times; premarital relations were met with the options of labeling & ostracizing the women, to stoning both parties. This man (Joseph), discovers that his wife-to-be (Mary) is pregnant, and he wasn't the birth father. What to do? Apparently, Joseph was struggling with the decision when he was confronted by an angel. Fear would be too slight a word for the reaction to this encounter, I think. The same would go for Mary, finding out about the pregnancy from an angel. This was one of those God things that would change both their lives forever.

The point of the story is as follows:
- Many of our fears are unfounded, unnecessary, and illogical.
- Many of our fears can be settled by God's Word.
- Many of our fears hold us back from fulfilling God's purposes.

BIBLE STUDY

<u>Joseph's Fear</u>

Matthew 1:18-25

Now the birth of Jesus Christ was on this wise: When as his mother Mary was espoused to Joseph, before they came together, she was found with child of the Holy Ghost. Then Joseph her husband, being a just man, and not willing to make her a public example, was minded to put her away privily.

While he thought on these things, behold, the angel of the Lord appeared unto him in a dream, saying:

- Joseph, thou son of David, fear not to take unto thee Mary thy wife for that which is conceived in her is of the Holy Ghost.
- And she shall bring forth a son, and thou shalt call his name Jesus for he shall save his people from their sins.

Now all this was done, that it might be fulfilled which was spoken of the Lord by the prophet, saying:

- Behold, a virgin shall be with child, and shall bring forth a son, and they shall call his name Emmanuel, which being interpreted is, God with us.

Then Joseph being raised from sleep did as the angel of the Lord had bidden him and took unto him his wife and knew her not till, she had brought forth her firstborn son and he called his name Jesus.

<u>Mary's Fear</u>
Luke 1:28-35

The angel came in unto her and said:
- Hail, thou that art highly favored, the Lord is with thee, blessed art thou among women.

When she saw him, she was troubled at his saying and cast in her mind what manner of salutation this should be. And the angel said unto her:
- Fear not, Mary, for thou hast found favor with God.
- Behold, thou shalt conceive in thy womb and bring forth a son, and shalt call his name Jesus.
- He shall be great and shall be called the Son of the Highest and the Lord God shall give unto him the throne of his father David.
- He shall reign over the house of Jacob forever; and of his kingdom there shall be no end.

Then said Mary unto the angel:
- How shall this be, seeing I know not a man?

The angel answered and said unto her:
- The Holy Ghost shall come upon thee, and the power of the Highest shall overshadow thee. Therefore, also that holy thing which shall be born of thee shall be called the Son of God.

Please answer the following questions:
- How would you act if confronted by an angel?
  - How would you respond
  - What would you believe?

BOLAND

FEARS

Jesus

Most people do not realize that Jesus had his scared to death moment.[xx] It wasn't at Lazarus' grave, it was while He was praying in the garden of Gethsemane, knowing His destiny. Luke wrote that an angel came and ministered to Him in His time of need.

All this occurred while:
- The disciples slept,
- The crowds left Him,
- The religious leaders plotted against Him,
- Just before Judas delivered Him.

It occurred prior to:
- The humiliation of a so-called trial,
- The presentation before Pilate,
- The beating & scourging by the Romans,
- The shame of crucifixion.

The worst part though was when God turned His back on Him as He became the perfect sacrificial lamb to cover the sins of the world!

The point of the story is as follows:
- Knowing your responsibility is sometimes frightening.
- Being human has its moments of short-term anxiety.
- Jesus understands our emotions.

BIBLE STUDY

<u>Jesus at Gethsemane</u>

Matthew 26:36-46

Then cometh Jesus with them unto a place called Gethsemane, and saith unto the disciples:
- Sit here, while I go and pray.

He took with him Peter and the two sons of Zebedee and began to be sorrowful and very heavy. Then saith he unto them:
- My soul is exceeding sorrowful, even unto death: tarry here, and watch with me.

He went a little farther, and fell on his face, and prayed, saying:
- My Father, if it be possible, let this cup pass from me, nevertheless, not as I will, but as thou wilt.

He come unto the disciples, found them asleep and saith unto Peter:
- What, could ye not watch with me one hour?
- Watch and pray, that you enter not into temptation.
- The spirit indeed is willing, but the flesh is weak.

He went away again the second time, and prayed, saying:
- My Father, if this cup may not pass away from me, except I drink it, thy will be done.

He came and found them asleep again for their eyes were heavy. He left them, went away again, and prayed the third time saying the same words.

Then cometh He to his disciples, and saith unto them:
- Sleep on now and take your rest.
- Behold, the hour is at hand,
- The Son of man is betrayed into the hands of sinners.
- Rise, let us be going.
- Behold, he is at hand that doth betray me.

Luke 22:43-45

There appeared an angel unto him from heaven, strengthening him. Being in an agony he prayed more earnestly:
- His sweat was as it were great drops of blood falling down to the ground.

When He rose up from prayer, and was come to His disciples, He found them sleeping for sorrow...

<u>Jesus on the Cross</u>

Matthew 27:46

About the ninth hour Jesus cried with a loud voice, saying:
- Eli, Eli, lama sabachthani?
  That is to say:
- My God, My God, why hast thou forsaken me?

Please answer the following questions:
- Knowing that Jesus had His moment (with good cause) and overcame it,
  - Should that help calm any fears we might have?
- The angels ministered to Him,
  - Does that give us hope that angels minister to us during our times of uncertainty?

FEARS

The Multitude

All those people who followed after Jesus watched in awe and wonder as:

- Jesus cured the sick,
- Jesus healed the disabled,
- Jesus raised the dead,
- Jesus taught with authority.

Many were actually scared to death of Him because they did not understand or know how to respond to someone who was so totally different. Jesus assured them that God cared and was there to make a difference in their lives.

- Some in the crowd,
  - Walked away from Him out of fear.
- A few in the crowd,
  - Simply asked to be left alone.
- Many in the crowd,
  - Only followed at a safe distance.
- Then out of the crowd came the curious
  - But were not committed followers.
- Finally, too many in the crowd,
  - Were afraid of community reaction to admit they would follow & believe.

The point of the story is as follows:
- Fear limits commitment.
- Fear is a reaction to the unknown.
- Knowledge breaks down fear.

BIBLE STUDY

<u>The Multitude Following Jesus</u>

Luke 8:36-38

They (multitude) also which saw it, told them by what means He that was possessed of the devils was healed. Then the whole multitude of the country of the Gadarenes round about besought Him to depart from them for they were taken with great fear. He went up into the ship and returned back again. Now the man out of whom the devils were departed besought Him that he (the healed man) might be with Him, but Jesus sent him away, saying,

- Return to thine own house,
- Show how great things God hath done unto thee.
  - He went his way
  - Published throughout the whole city how great things Jesus had done unto him.

Acts 2:43

Fear came upon every soul and many wonders and signs were done by the apostles.

Please answer the following questions:

- Does God's Word scare you?
- Does Jesus' story sound unbelievable?
- If you answered yes to either question:
  - Should you seek the assistance of someone mature in God's Word to help you understand its concepts & meaning?

BOLAND

FEARS

The Disciples

Apparently, the Disciples were afraid of many things:
- Of Jesus' power & authority.
- Of the control of the Pharisees & Sadducees.
- Of the influence of the crowd.

They were strong while Jesus was with them, but immediately after the crucifixion and early in the book of Acts, they were without their leader. He was executed in the most public and excruciating manner possible. The dream, the ministry and their hopes were dead.

They feared for their lives!
- Would the religious authorities come after them too?
- Would they be the next in line to see the Roman justice?

They coward in an unassuming building. They attempted to walk stealthily unnoticed through the Jerusalem crowds. It wasn't until the appearance of the resurrected Lord Himself that self-assurance, confidence, and boldness of the resurrection was restored to this small band of Galilean misfits. Jesus made the difference in their countenance. The indwelling of the Holy Spirit made the difference in their boldness to become witnesses for Christ and the message of the Gospel and the Word of God.

The point of the story is as follows:
- Fear does not stop loss, it stops living.
- Worry doesn't take away tomorrow's problems, it takes away today's peace.

BOLAND

BIBLE STUDY

<u>Of Jesus</u>

Luke 5:9-11 (MSG)

Simon Peter, when he saw it, fell to his knees before Jesus.

- Master, leave. I'm a sinner and can't handle this holiness. Leave me to myself.

When they pulled in that catch of fish, awe overwhelmed Simon and everyone with him. It was the same with James and John, Zebedee's sons, coworkers with Simon.

Jesus said to Simon:
- There is nothing to fear.
- From now on you'll be fishing for men and women.
- They pulled their boats up on the beach, left them, nets and all, and followed him.

<u>In the Boat</u>

Matthew 8:23-27; Mark 4:35-41; Luke 8:22-25

And when he was entered into a ship, His disciples followed him. Behold, there arose a great tempest in the sea, insomuch that the ship was covered with the waves:
- But He (Jesus) was asleep.

His disciples came to Him, and awoke Him, saying:
- Lord, save us, we perish.

He saith unto them:
- Why are you fearful?
- O you of little faith?

Then He arose, and rebuked the winds and the sea:
- And there was a great calm.

The men marveled, saying:
- What manner of man is this, that even the winds and the sea obey Him!

<u>Disciples after Jesus crucifixion</u>

John 20:19-20

Then the same day at evening, being the first day of the week, when the doors were shut. The disciples were assembled for fear of the Jews. Then came Jesus and stood in the midst and saith unto them:
- Peace be unto you.
- Then He showed them His hands and side.

<u>Peter & John Beaten</u>

Acts 5:38-42

And now I (Gamaliel) say unto you, Refrain from these men, and let them alone for if this counsel:
- If this work be of men,
  - it will come to naught.
- If it be of God,
  - You cannot overthrow it.

- o Lest happily you be found even to fight against God.

And to him they agreed:
- They (The Council) called the apostles,
- They beat them,
- They commanded that they should not speak in the name of Jesus and let them go.

Then they (Peter & John) departed from the presence of the council,
- Rejoicing that they were counted worthy to suffer shame for His (Jesus) name.
- [They continued] daily in the temple, and in every house,
- They ceased not to teach and preach Jesus Christ.

Please answer the following questions:
- If Christ is for us why do we yield to fear?
- Can belief in the power of Christ overcome fear?

FEARS

Early Believers

Joseph of Arimathea

He was considered a good and just man who did not consent to the treatment or trial of Jesus.[xxi] He was an early believer plus a prominent member of the Council. Matthew, Mark, Luke, and John wrote about him gathering up courage and going before Pilate to ask for the body of Jesus.[xxii] He secretly feared retribution from the other Jewish leaders on the council because of his strong stance on the matter of Jesus as the Christ. According to all accounts, he placed the body of Jesus in his newly fashion unused tomb.

Nicodemus

Nicodemus was afraid, maybe even ashamed to be seen with Christ, therefore came in the night.[xxiii] John wrote about that visit and conversation with Jesus.[xxiv] It does seems odd that only John wrote about this event. Maybe it was because the other gospel writers were protecting Nicodemus from unwanted notoriety which would get him in trouble with the ruling council because he believed in Christ.

It was a well-known fact that Nicodemus was a Pharisee & member of the Sanhedrin. [xxv] As a Pharisee he believed in a resurrection. As a Pharisee he was responsible for religious legalism. Apparently, by the time of Jesus death, he was no longer afraid of his standing among these authorities. The record shows that he helped Joseph of Arimathea retrieve Jesus' body!

Ananias & Sapphira

Ananias, along with his wife Sapphira sold a piece of land but did not give the entire proceed to the church. However, they claimed what they gave was the full amount. When confronted about it, he fell down dead and so did his wife. Word spread fast about what happened and people feared the power of the disciples' power and abilities.

<u>The Early Church</u>

After Pentecost, things happened fast. Those coming to belief in Jesus Christ were in absolute terror of the many signs and wonders being done by the disciples. These uneducated fisherman from Galilee, could:

- Converse with people who spoke in different languages about Jesus,
- Were released from prison by angels,
- Healed the sick and blind,
- Even watched people die instantly,
  - Who lied to the Holy Spirit!

As new believers matured in their faith, Jesus Christ settled and calmed their fears and anxiety.

<table>
<tr><td>

The point of the story is as follows:
- Our importance & standing in the community is not important to Christ.
- Fear is conquered when confronted by the Spirit of God.
- God's Will overcomes our emotions

</td></tr>
</table>

BIBLE STUDY

Matthew 27:56-58; Mark 15:42-44; Luke 23:50-53;
John 19:37-39

Among which was Mary Magdalene, and Mary the mother of James and Joses, and the mother of Zebedee's children. When the even was come, there came a rich man of Arimathea, named Joseph, who also himself was Jesus' disciple. He went to Pilate and begged the body of Jesus. Then Pilate commanded the body to be delivered.

Mark 15:45

And when he (Pilate) knew it (the death of Jesus) of the centurion, he gave the body to Joseph.

Luke 23:53

And he (Joseph) took it down (the body of Jesus), and wrapped it in linen, and laid it in a sepulcher that was hewn in stone, wherein never man before was laid.

John 3:1-3

There was a man of the Pharisees, named Nicodemus, a ruler of the Jews. The same came to Jesus by night, and said unto him:
- Rabbi, we know that thou art a teacher come from God for no man can do these miracles that thou do, except God be with him.

John19:39

And there also came Nicodemus, which at the first came to Jesus by night, and brought a mixture of myrrh and aloes, about a hundred-pound weight.

Acts 5:1-11

A certain man named Ananias, with Sapphira his wife, sold a possession and kept back part of the price, his wife also being privy to it, and brought a certain part, and laid it at the apostles' feet.

Peter said:
- Ananias, why hath Satan filled thine heart to lie to the Holy Ghost,
- To keep back part of the price of the land,
- Whiles it remained, was it not thine own,
- After it was sold, was it not in thine own power,
- Why hast thou conceived this thing in thine heart?
- Thou hast not lied unto men, but unto God!

Ananias hearing these words fell down and gave up the ghost and great fear came on all them that heard these things. The young men arose wound him up and carried him out and buried him.

It was about the space of three hours after, when his wife, not knowing what was done, came in.
Peter answered unto her:
- Tell me whether you sold the land for so much?

And she said,
- Yea, for so much.

Then Peter said unto her:
- How is it that ye have agreed together to tempt the Spirit of the Lord?
- Behold, the feet of them which have buried thy husband are at the door and shall carry thee out.

Then fell she down straightway at his feet and yielded up the ghost. The young men came in, found her dead and carrying her forth buried her by her husband.

A great fear came upon all the church and upon as many as heard these things.

Please answer the following questions:
- How strong is your faith?
- Could your faith stand up to public scrutiny?
- What would be the condition of the church today if liars were treated like Ananias & Sapphira?

FEARS

Saul to Paul

Paul of Tarshish was a young, brash, and confident Pharisee who was carrying out the bidding of the Sanhedrin to eliminate the Jesus movement wherever he found it. He was on his way to deal with the movement in Damascus when he had a life changing, personal encounter with the person of Jesus Christ himself. This Jesus moment not only brought him to his knees and scared him to death but changed the direction of his ministry.

At first he had to convince the very people he once persecuted of the experience he had and the inner change, then he had to realize that he would have to put up with the thought that now he would be persecuted.

The point of the story is as follows:
- When God calls there is no going back.
- A true God moment is life changing.
- A true God movement cannot be stopped!

BIBLE STUDY

Acts 8:1-3

Saul was consenting unto his death. And at that time there was a great persecution against the church which was at Jerusalem; and they were all scattered abroad throughout the regions of Judaea and Samaria, except the apostles. And devout men carried Stephen to his burial and made great lamentation over him. As for Saul, he made havoc of the church, entering into every house, and hauling off men and women committed them to prison.

Acts 9:1-6

Saul, yet breathing out threatening and slaughter against the disciples of the Lord, went unto the high priest and desired of him letters to Damascus to the synagogues, that if he found any of this way, whether they were men or women, he might bring them bound unto Jerusalem. As he journeyed, he came near Damascus: and suddenly there shined round about him a light from heaven:

He fell to the earth, heard a voice saying unto him:
* Saul, Saul, why persecute thou Me?

He said:
* Who art thou, Lord?

The Lord said:
- I am Jesus whom thou persecute.
- It is hard for thee to kick against the pricks.

He trembling and astonished said:
- Lord, what wilt thou have me to do?

The Lord said unto him:
- Arise, and go into the city,
- It shall be told thee what thou must do.

Please answer the following questions:
- Why would God use a man who persecuted the church?
- When God calls you out what should your response be?

BOLAND

FEARS

The Roman Captain

The Captain of the guard was about to beat Paul until they found out that he was a privileged Roman citizen. The Jews in Jerusalem were targeting Paul for death due to his conversion to following the way of Jesus. The Captain once realizing his error stopped the activity because it was more of a crime to beat a citizen of Rome than satisfy the appetite for revenge of the Jews. He was afraid he had made a serious error. He saved Paul:

- From a serious beating.
- From the Jewish leaders.
- For God's purpose in Rome.

The point of the story is as follows:
- God sometimes uses emotions for His purposes.
- Fear isn't always a negative if we see the good that can come out of it.

BIBLE STUDY

Acts 22:24-29

The chief captain commanded him to be brought into the castle and bade that he should be examined by scourging; that he might know wherefore they cried so against him. As they bound him with thongs,

Paul said unto the centurion that stood by:
- Is it lawful for you to scourge a man that is a Roman, and uncondemned?

When the centurion heard that, he went and told the chief captain, saying:
- Take heed what thou do for this man is a Roman.

Then the chief captain came, and said unto him:
- Tell me, art thou a Roman?
  He said,
- Yea.

The chief captain answered:
- With a great sum obtained I this freedom.
  Paul said:
- I was free born.

Then straightway they departed from him which should have examined him and the chief captain also was afraid after he knew that he was a Roman and because he had bound him.

Acts 23:10-11

When there arose a great dissension, the chief captain, fearing lest Paul should have been pulled in pieces of them, commanded the soldiers to go down, and to take him by force from among them, and to bring him into the castle.

The night following the Lord stood by him (Paul), and said,
- Be of good cheer, Paul,
- For as thou hast testified of Me in Jerusalem,
- So, must thou bear witness also at Rome.

Please answer the following questions:
- Have you ever had a life changing event which you know God used?
- If yes, has it produced a ministry to others?
  - Why or why not?

FEARS

CONCLUSION

When life seems emotionally out of control, where do you go? When anxiety takes over, to whom do you turn? Since the beginning of time God's people have faced life's emotional roller coaster: life events, disasters, health issues, job losses, etc. The experiences and testimony left by biblical characters help us understand ways to respond. The response can be two-fold: worldly or faith in God.

In this modern society we face even more pressure like the possibilities of mass killings, workplace violence, loss of livelihood, pandemics, financial crisis, loss of family, and even disease. Imagine any one of these things happening to someone close to you, or maybe you don't have to imagine. Just remember the biblical heroes of the past and how they dealt with:

- Selfishness & lived to regret it,
    - Yet God cares in spite of the conduct.
- Banishment & selfish conduct,
    - Yet, God protects life anyway.
- Unfulfilled promises,
    - Yet, God's promises took care of individuals & family throughout life.
- Laughing at the Word of God,
    - Yet, God blesses and fulfills His promises in spite of conduct.

- Feared the people because of a lifestyle of thievery & lying,
  - Yet, God stays and guides anyway.
- A life begun in slavery ending in royalty.
  - All the while God blessed, protected, and used in spite of conditions.
- A lifestyle based on fear,
  - Yet, God used that life for His purpose in spite of the emotion.
- The doubt & the fear,
  - Yet, God stayed true in spite of an attitude of unfaithfulness.
- An attitude of unworthiness, being unprepared, and unqualified,
  - Yet, God plan succeeded anyway.
- A lifetime of loss & bitterness,
  - Yet, God blessed anyway.
- Forcibly removed from homeland, family & comfortable surroundings,
  - Yet, God blessed the loyalty, honesty, & faithfulness.
- Lost fortune, children and accused of heresy by friends & family,
  - Yet, God was faithful to restore health and fortune because of faithfulness.

- Forgot God,
  - o Yet, God never left in spite negative emotions.
- Disobey God and did not regret it,
  - o Yet, God stayed true.
- Feared man over God, violate God's commandment,
  - o Yet, God sought a relationship.
- Lived a hard life of insults, beatings, jail, & prisons,
  - o Yet, God protected and used mightily.
- Lost family, homeland, manhood and got punish for believing,
  - o Yet, God used & gave a vision of the future.
- Lost everything,
  - o Yet, God used faithfulness in spite how others attempted to discredit a witness for God.
- Tried to run from God,
  - o Yet, God uses mightily in bringing others to repentance.
  - o God used the fear in mighty ways.
- Personally, considered fearful, anxiety and unqualified,
  - o Yet, God used to His glory.
- Filled with fear, anxiety, and doubts,
  - o Yet, God used to spread the word about Jesus beyond their wildest dreams.
- Unable to overcome fears, anxiety, and disbelief,
  - o Yet, God used it all to His purpose.
- Considered fearful, and unavailable,
  - o Yet, God instilled courage, and faithfulness in order to see Jesus vision.

So, this is their stories and God's results. What is your story as life turns upside down to the point it becomes unrecognizable? It goes without saying that we will experience such emotions as: fear, anxiety, pain, sorrow, insecurity, & self-doubt. How life turns out at that point is determined by how you handle these setbacks and deal with these emotions. What do you do?

- Do you deny these emotions?
- Do you express grief?
- Do you go full blown ballistic?
- Do you tear your clothes?
- Do you shave your head?
- Or, as a child in the grocery store fall to the ground and have a temper tantrum?

As believers our only hope in dealing with a wide range of emotions is to seek God, honor God, & praise God. Like the heroes of the Scriptures we should acknowledged God's gifts and worship Him.

- Yes, we can have a bazillion questions for God.
- Yes, we can take them directly to God.
- Yes, we can have serious doubts about our abilities.
    - However, at the same time know that we can do all things through Christ who strengthens us![xxvi]

Jesus promised his disciples an encouragement and peace amid the turmoil. Jesus promised:

- In this world you will have trouble.
- In me (Jesus) I have overcome the world. [xxvii]

If you haven't already, you should know that we will face varying degrees of emergencies or problems in this life, many of them will also turn into a crisis of faith.[xxviii] The book of Hebrews says that faith is the substance of things hoped for and the evidence of things not seen.[xxix] The crisis comes when our emotions over take our faith in not believing that which we know to be true and fail to understand it because we don't see it! Yet, behind the scenes is God, an available source of hope and stability. He is there to take us to a future that is beyond our wildest dreams which brings glory and honor to Him. We make this future unattainable and unavailable if we let our emotions control our state of mind, our relations with others, or our general conduct & attitude.

Final warning: God cautions us in the book of Proverbs that if we take lightly His counsel, ignore, or change His Words in Scripture, then when heartache, calamity, or problems come; He will not hear our prayers or answer them.[xxx]

When someone is afraid of unknown future events it usually means they have not come to grips with the one who controls those events. One of the oldest questions' humankind has been asking is,

"Who is God and how can I know Him?"

According to Scripture, the answer is an easy one. God wants a relationship but humankind chose to do the opposite and sin poisoned the world. Sin separated us from God not the other way around. Everything changed after that.

- Romans 3:23 says,

  For all have sinned and fall short of the glory of God.

- Isaiah 59:2 says,

  Your iniquities have separated between you and your God, and your sins have hid His face from you, that He will not hear.

We have been trying to earn our way back to God ever since then. We have tried by being good people. We have tried through religion, money, morality, philosophy, education, any number of ways. Nothing seems to work.

- Proverbs 14:12 says,

    There is a way which seems right unto a man,

    but the end thereof are the ways of death.

Scriptures tells us that there is only one way to find peace with God, and that is through Jesus Christ.

- Romans 5:8 says,

    But God commended His love toward us, in that,

    while we were yet sinners, Christ died for us.

So, this is the how we overcome our fears and restore our relationship with God. Even though we were still on the outs with God, Jesus came to earth, died on the cross and pay the price for our sins so that we could have a restored relationship with God through Him.

- John 3:16 says,

    For God so loved the world, that He gave his only begotten Son, that whosoever believes in Him should not perish, but have everlasting life.

- John 5:24 says,

  I say unto you, He that heareth My word, and believeth on Him that sent Me, hath everlasting life, and shall not come into condemnation; but is passed from death unto life

- John 10:10b says,

  I am come that they might have life, and that they might have it more abundantly.

- Romans 5:1 says,

- *Therefore, being justified by faith, we have peace with God through our Lord Jesus Christ:*

- 1 Samuel 16:7b says,

  The Lord sees not as man sees:

  For man looks on the outward appearance,

  But the Lord looks on the heart

You may ask how can a person have peace in the middle of their fears?[xxxi]

1. If they are not a believer, they must first admit that you are a sinner and fall short of the glory of God.

2. Then they must believe that Jesus Christ died for their sins on the cross and rose from the grave, conquering death, and sin.

3. After that they must invite Jesus Christ to live in their heart and be the Lord of their life, accepting His free gift of eternal life.

4. Then, they must voice their fears before God.

    a. Turning them over to God and not taking them back.

5. They must be strong and brave because the devil is just waiting to place doubt in their mind and put fear back in their life!

    - Ephesians 4:27

      Neither give place to the devil.

    - James 4:7

      Submit yourselves therefore to God.

      Resist the devil, and he will flee from you.

    - 1 Peter 5:8

      Be sober, be vigilant, because your adversary the devil, as a roaring lion, walketh about, seeking whom he may devour:

BOLAND

FEARS

BIBLIOGRAPHY

---

[i] https://www.psychologytoday.com/us/basics/fear
[ii] 1 John 4:18
[iii] *The Psychology Behind Fear,* By Lisa Fritscher
Medically reviewed by Steven Gans, MD, April 03, 2020
https://www.verywellmind.com/the-psychology-of-fear-2671696
[iv] *Dissecting terror: How does fear work?* By Tim Newman (October 31, 2018) Fact checked by Jasmin Collier
https://www.medicalnewstoday.com/articles/323492
[v] https://www.merriam-webster.com/dictionary/fear
[vi] Mayo Foundation for Medical Education and Research (MFMER).
https://www.mayoclinic.org/diseases-conditions/anxiety/symptoms-causes/syc-20350961
https://www.mayoclinic.org/search/search-results?q=fear
[vii] Anxiety and Depression Association of America
National Institute of Mental Health
World Health Organization: Mental Health
https://adaa.org/about-adaa/press-room/facts-statistics
[viii] Earl E. Bakken Center for Spirituality & Healing
https://www.takingcharge.csh.umn.edu/impact-fear-and-anxiety
[ix] Job 28:28
[x] 1 John 4:18, Matthew 10:28, Psalm 2:11, 34:7, 55:19, 56:4, 111:10, 112:1, 115:11, 147:11; Proverbs 3:25, Romans 8:14-16
[xi] Proverbs 1:7, 26-27, 29
[xii] Psalm 34:7
[xiii] Romans 3:18

[xiv] http://www.prisonhistory.net/
https://www.ancient-origins.net/history-ancient-traditions/prisons-and-imprisonment-ancient-world-punishments-used-maintain-public-020588
https://www.bible-history.com/sketches/ancient/binding-prisoners.html

---

xv 2 Corinthians 1:3-4

xvi Judges 7

xviihttps://pjcc.org/jewish-life/jewish-holidays-explained/shavuot/

xviii Ezekiel 23:40; 2 Samuel 12:20; Leviticus 14:8-9; 15:5-6, 18, 19-24, 31; 16:4

xix myjewishlearning.com

xx Matthew 26:37-38; Luke 22:44

xxi Luke 23:50-52,

xxiiMark 15:43; John 19:38
https://www.whatchristianswanttoknow.com/whatever-happened-to-nicodemus-and-joseph-of-arimathea/#ixzz6KdStZlK2

xxiii *Matthew Henry Commentary*, Edited by Leslie F. Church, Zondervan Publishing, Grand Rapids, MI, 1961
P1517

xxiv John 3:1-2

xxvhttps://www.whatchristianswanttoknow.com/whatever-happened-to-nicodemus-and-joseph-of-arimathea/#ixzz6KdTNRl6G

xxvi Philippians 4:13

xxvii John 16:7,33

xxviii YouVersion Bible reading plan, "Trusting God in the Storm" by Elliot Williams for The Navigators.

xxix Hebrews 11:1

xxx Proverbs 1:25-28

xxxi The Bridge to Life ©1976 The Navigators, all rights reserved.